Leonard Schneider
117 W. Genesee St.
Lansing, Mich.

Nov. 12, 1930

ALFRED LORD TENNYSON

𝔐errill's 𝔈nglish 𝔗exts

TENNYSON'S
IDYLLS OF THE KING

THE COMING OF ARTHUR
GARETH AND LYNETTE
LANCELOT AND ELAINE
THE HOLY GRAIL
GUINEVERE
THE PASSING OF ARTHUR

EDITED WITH AN INTRODUCTION AND NOTES BY
W. D. LEWIS, M. A., PRINCIPAL OF THE WILLIAM
PENN HIGH SCHOOL FOR GIRLS, PHILADELPHIA

NEW YORK
CHARLES E. MERRILL COMPANY

CONTENTS

INTRODUCTION

ALFRED TENNYSON

BIOGRAPHICAL details become valuable only when their study is prompted by interest in an author's work. Then the literature and the man present a unified message, particularly in the case of an author like Tennyson, whose life and personality are so completely identified with his utterances that a study of the man involves thorough acquaintance with his poetry.

Alfred Tennyson was born in 1809. His parentage and environment were favorable to the training of a literary artist. His father was a cultured and scholarly clergyman who gave much of his time to the education of his children. Dr. Henry Van Dyke says: "The doors of the ideal world were opened to them very early; they were encouraged to imagine as well as to think; they peopled their play-grounds with lofty visions of kings and knights, and fought out the world-old battles of right and wrong in their childish games, and wove their thoughts of virtue and courage and truth into long romances with which they entertained each other in turn at the dinner-table."

Under his father's instruction Tennyson became a first rate classical scholar. He absorbed from Greek literature a wealth of imagery and allusion that is frequently in evidence in his poetry. More important, probably, was the Greek contribution to his unerring feeling for the right effect, in word, phrase, and rhythm. To Greek nature worship he added the modern scientific appreciation of the wonders of the universe. In these early years he also became so familiar with Shakespeare, Milton, Pope, Goldsmith, Addison, Bunyan, and other great English writers that he constantly measured his own art by the best standards and drew inspiration from loving companionship with the greatest teachers.

He was continually trying his boyish hand at writing poetry. A quotation from the poet himself in the *Memoir* says: "About ten or eleven Pope's *Homer's Iliad* became a favorite of mine and I wrote hundreds and hundreds of lines in the regular Popeian metre, nay even could improvise them. . . . At about twelve and onward I wrote an epic of six thousand lines à la Walter Scott. Though the performance was very likely worth nothing, I never felt myself more truly inspired."

In 1828 he entered Trinity College, Cambridge. Here he lived much with a group of friends called "the Apostles," many of whom became distinguished men. In 1829 he won the Chancellor's prize for a poem entitled "Timbuctoo." He took great interest in politics, always sympathizing with the popular party. Indeed, so strong a partisan was he that with his friend Hallam he made a trip to the Pyrenees to carry money to a party in revolt against the Spanish government.

In 1831 his college career was interrupted by the illness of his father, whose death a little later placed the care of his mother and sister upon him. The family fortune made it possible, however, for him to devote himself to poetry, and to these early years belong some of his best known poems, including "The Lady of Shalott," "The Palace of Art," "The May Queen," and "The Lotus Eaters," published in the volume of 1832.

The death of his friend Arthur Henry Hallam in 1833 was a shock that nearly unbalanced his faith. For about ten years he produced very little poetry. These were years of mental and spiritual adjustment, of careful self-education, and of searching self-criticism. His engagement to Emily Sellwood helped to restore his harmony with the order of the universe and furnished him with a motive for renewed activity. In 1842 he published two volumes which contained many of his best poems. The excellence of his work was at once recognized by the reviewers and by the great writers of the day. In 1845 he was awarded the public recognition of a pension of £200 per annum. The publication of *The Princess* in 1847 and of *In Memoriam* in 1850 gave him the assurance of an income that warranted his marriage to Miss Sellwood, which occurred in June, 1850. Upon the death of Wordsworth in the same year he was appointed poet laureate.

From this time to his death in 1892 Tennyson was the most prominent figure in English letters. While he was intimate with the greatest men of his age, he shunned publicity and hated flattery. His modesty was well illustrated by his reluctant acceptance of the peerage in 1884 after he had thrice refused the honor. His time was spent mostly at his beautiful home, Farringford, in the Isle of Wight, where he could hear

"The league-long roller thundering on the reef,"

or at his summer home at Aldworth in Surrey. No author of his generation worked more assiduously to give full expression to his muse. His greatest works, *In Memoriam* and *The Idylls of the King*, were the products of many years of the most painstaking workmanship. In everything that he wrote he displayed the most consummate art; indeed he may be called the supreme artist of our literature.

Tennyson's personal appearance suggested the inspired bard. Thomas Carlyle thus describes him:

"One of the finest looking men in the world. A great shock of rough dusky dark hair; bright, laughing, hazel eyes; massive aquiline face, most massive yet most delicate; of sallow brown complexion, almost Indian looking, clothes cynically loose, free-and-easy, smokes infinite tobacco. His voice is musical, metallic, fit for loud laughter and piercing wail, and all that may lie between; speech and speculation free and plenteous; I do not meet in these late decades such company over a pipe! we shall see what he will grow to."

THE ARTHURIAN LEGEND

Although they have much in common with the mythological hero-tales of Greece and Rome, there is probably a historical basis for the legends of Arthur and his Round Table. Beyond the fact, however, that the hero was a leader of the Celtic tribes who beat back the Saxon invaders early in the sixth century, the investigator finds little that is authentic. In his scholarly study, *The Growth of the Idylls of the King*, Dr. Richard Jones says:

"But the struggle with the Teutonic invaders, however bravely and desperately fought, was in vain. As the cause of the highly-gifted, imaginative Celt became more and more hopelessly crushed in conflict with the kinsmen of the conquerors of Rome, he found solace in song for the hard facts of life. He won in the fields of imagination the victories denied him on the field of battle, and he clustered these triumphs against the enemies of his race about the name and the person of the magnanimous Arthur. By the Norman conquest of England the heart of the Celtic world was profoundly stirred. Ancient memories awoke, and, yearning for the restoration of British greatness, men rehearsed the deeds of him who had been king, and of whom it was prophesied that he should be king hereafter.

"Geoffrey of Monmouth wrote about 1132–35 A. D. (Ten Brink) a history of Britain in Latin, a book which, whatever its faults as a history, was an epoch-making book, because, though it did not originate the Arthur legends, it yet made them radiant with poetic coloring, and thus contributed toward making them that which they soon became, the common property of Europe. Geoffrey's book, still characterized as a work of genius and of imagination, is the source of a stream of poetry that flows to our day. It was forthwith translated into French by Wace, who added the story of the Round Table. Within a generation or two innumerable versions, into which had been woven the legend of the Holy Grail, appeared among the principal nations of Europe, two of the more prominent writers being Chrestien de

Troyes in France, and in Germany Wolfram von Eschenbach with his 'Parzival,' later the theme of Wagner's greatest opera."

The wandering minstrels did much to spread these legends and to give them infinite variety of form. In their hands they came to represent the varying ideals of different peoples and of successive ages. Their influence is thus explained by Ten Brink in his *History of English Literature:*

"But herein lies the essential difference between that age and our own: the result of poetical activity was not the property and not the production of a single person, but *of the community*. The work of the individual singer endured only as long as its delivery lasted. He gained personal distinction only as a virtuoso. The permanent elements of what he presented, the material, the ideas, even the style and metre, already existed. The work of the singer was only a ripple in *the stream of national poetry*. Who can say how much the individual contributed to it, or where in his poetical recitation memory ceased and creative impulse began! In any case the work of the individual lived on only as the ideal possession of the aggregate body of the people, and it soon lost the stamp of originality."

Happily it is not our problem to trace the variations of these stories, nor to classify the various cycles of legend that in time entered into the complete mass. One element that had great influence in giving these romances increased popularity and added dignity was the introduction of the legend of the Holy Grail. Tennyson makes the Holy Grail—

> "The cup, the cup itself, from which our Lord
> Drank at the last sad supper with his own;"

although some other versions make it "the dish which held the paschal lamb at the Last Supper," or "the vessel in which Joseph of Arimathea had received the Savior's blood." In any case it represented the doctrine of transubstantiation, and, becoming a part of a popular tradition, it served as a means of doctrinal teaching. The legends accordingly received the sanction of the church, "whose spiritual rulers made the minstrel doubly welcome when celebrating this theme."

During successive ages, the great mine of poetic material formed by these tales has furnished suggestion and inspiration to the poets of many lands who have transmuted its ores into the precious metals of their genius. Dante, Spenser, Shakespeare, Milton, Dryden, Scott, Wordsworth, Swinburne, Lowell, and many others have treated themes drawn from this source.

The most important compilation of these legends is that of Sir Thomas Malory, entitled *Morte D'Arthur*, which was first published in 1485. To this book Tennyson was chiefly indebted, although his version of the stories varies widely from the original. Indeed, it may be said that like the ancient bards, Tennyson has adapted the legends to his own day, so that we have a sixth-century historical setting, a mediæval chivalry, and nineteenth-century social ideals.

THE GROWTH OF THE IDYLLS

The growth of the Idylls in the poet's mind was not unlike their original development. Early in life he was fascinated by Malory's book, and throughout one of the longest of modern literary careers, "what he called 'the greatest of all poetical subjects' perpetually haunted him." His first poem growing out of this interest is "The Lady of Shalott," published in 1832, a foreshadowing of "Lancelot and Elaine."

The volume of his poems published ten years later bore evidence of his continued interest in the Arthurian romances in the poems, "Sir Galahad," "Sir Launcelot and Queen Guinevere," and "Morte d'Arthur," the last of which forms a part of the present poem, "The Passing of Arthur." The first edition of *The Idylls of the King* appeared in 1859, containing "Enid," "Vivien," "Elaine," and "Guinevere." In 1869 were published four more of the Idylls, "The Coming of Arthur," "The Holy Grail," "Pelleas and Ettarre," and "The Passing of Arthur," and in 1872, "Gareth and Lynette" and "The Last Tournament." In 1885 "Balin and Balan" was added. The division of "Enid" into "The Marriage of Geraint" and "Geraint and Enid" completes the cycle of twelve poems. The "Dedication" to the Prince Consort was published in 1862, and the epilogue "To the Queen," in 1873. Thus the complete epic grew: a part that now comes last appeared first, and other parts appeared at irregular intervals in much the promiscuous manner of the original legends.

The record of their publication shows the growth of the cycle of poems in the author's mind. The *Memoir* contains this quotation from the poet: "The vision of Arthur as I have drawn him had come upon me when, little more than a boy, I lighted on Malory." It was not until 1855 that the poet decided on their final form. The changes in text so carefully collated by Professor Jones in his book quoted on page 8 show the gradual evolution of the poet's plan through a lifetime of study and inspiration.

In their final form the Idylls are complete in action and unified in theme. They present a moral epic full of profound spiritual truth. The noble plan of Arthur's kingdom, founded on the highest ideals of social service, the portrayal of its triumphant righteousness in "Gareth and Lynette," the gradual demoralization of the purpose of Arthur's life through the sin of Lancelot and the Queen, down to the "Tournament of the Dead Innocence" where the false Lancelot sits in Arthur's chair to award the prize to the shameless Tristram amid a throng that in spiritual gloom acknowledges that the day of Innocence is past,—all this is told with profound insight into the fundamental laws of social structure and of individual character.

If the dramatic ending is tragic, it is illumined by spiritual hope. Lancelot, who never ceased to battle against the guilty love that "marr'd his face and mark'd it ere his time," dies a "holy man;" and the beautiful Queen responds to the powers that tend the soul, fortifies herself with the hope that in her own heart she can live down sin, and passes

> "To where beyond these voices there is peace."

Arthur himself fails to find God in his ways with men, but realizes that our human vision is dim

> "Perchance because we see not to the close."

And after reading the marvelous poetry describing the last, dim, weird battle in the death-white mist, it is with a sense of human triumph that we watch the lessening barge as it bears him—

> "To the island-valley of Avilion;
> Where falls not hail, or rain, or any snow,
> Nor ever wind blows loudly; but it lies
> Deep-meadow'd, happy, fair with orchard lawns
> And bowery hollows crown'd with summer sea."

THE VERSE STRUCTURE OF THE IDYLLS

Like many great English poems *The Idylls of the King* are written in blank verse, or unrimed iambic pentameter. In their peculiar delicacy, in their responsiveness to every mood, and in their subtle harmony of sound with movement and emotion, they have a distinct individuality. Of Tennyson's blank verse in these poems, Stopford Brooke says: "It is, as a vehicle of thought and emotion, entirely at the poet's command. He can make it do exactly what he likes. It has, at his choice, ease and rapidity, or slow and stately movement, or it echoes in its sound the thought, the scene, or the thing. It is by turns loud or low, soft or rough in spirit, fluid or rigid, abrupt, delayed, smooth, continuous, weighty and light."

The regular meter of the Idylls is iambic pentameter, or a verse consisting of five two-syllable feet, each foot an iambus, one composed of an unaccented followed by an accented syllable. The ordinary verse in this meter is scanned as follows: [1]

> Then rose'/Elaine'/ and glid'/ed thro''/ the fields',
> And past'/ beneath'/ the weird'/ly-sculp'/tured gates'
> > *L. E., 838–839.*

This meter is regular, the accent falling on each alternate syllable, beginning with the second. Tennyson varies from this standard form in many ways throughout the poems. It is not

---

[1] It cannot be too strongly insisted that the classification of vowels into *long* and *short* has absolutely nothing to do with stress in scansion. Vowels not marked are unaccented.

worth while to classify these changes. We may note, however, that he uses the following seven kinds of feet in addition to the *iambus:* the *trochee,* a foot of two syllables, the first of which is accented; the *spondee,* two syllables, both accented; the *pyrrhic,* two syllables, neither accented; the *dactyl,* three syllables, the first accented; the *anapest,* three syllables, the last accented; the *amphibrach,* three syllables, the second accented; and the *amphimacer,* three syllables, the first and the last accented.

A few illustrations may assist in cultivating a ready response to the poet's marvelous harmony of sound, sense, and emotion.

We feel Gareth's hesitation in

> Gar′eth / awhile′/ lin′ger′d. / The moth′/er′s eye′
>> *G. L., 169.*

There is a similar feeling in

> Down′ the/ long′ tow′/er stairs′/ hes′i/tat′ing.
>> *L. E., 341.*

Movement is wonderfully expressed in many passages, for example:

> Set lance′/ in rest,′/ strike′ spur,′/ sud′den/ly move,′
> Meet,′ in/ the midst,′/ and there′/ so fu′ri/ously
> Shock,′ that/ a man′/ far-off′/ might well′/ perceive,′
> If an′/y man′/ that day′/ were left′/ afield,′
> The hard′/ earth′ shake,′/ and a/ low′ thun′/der of arms.′
>> *L. E., 454–458.*

The deliberate preparation in the first line of this passage; the sharp decisive action in the two monosyllables of the spondee, *strike spur;* the forward lurch of the horses in the succeeding trochee and iambus, *suddenly move;* the apprehension in the first of the next line, *Meet in the midst;* the flutter in the pyrrhic at the end of this line; and the climax on the heavy stroke in the *Shock* at the beginning of the third line,—all contribute to an expressiveness that would give some sense of the action if the passage were well read to one entirely ignorant of English. With a rapid turn, the point of view is shifted and the first three stressed syllables of the last line, followed by the two successive strokes on the long vowels in *low thunder*, make us feel and hear the conflict as if from a distance.

Without further comment, the following lines may be taken as examples of the poet's skill in shifting emphasis, harmonizing sound with thought, or subtly suggesting an emotion that cannot be expressed in words:

but when the prince
Three' times'/ had blown'/—af'ter/long' hush'/—at last'
G. L., 1343.

And the/ long' glo'/ries of/ the win'/ter moon.'
P. A., 360.

Like this'/ last,' dim,'/ weird' bat'/tle of/ the west,'
P. A., 93.

The bare'/ black' cliffs'/ clang'd' round'/ him, as'/ he based.'
P. A., 356.

Immin'/gled with Heav'/en's az'/ure wa'/veringly,'
G. L., 914.

Mut'tering/ and mur'/muring at'/ his ear,'/ "Quick,' quick!"'
P. A., 347.

So strode' he/ back' slow'/ to the wound'/ed King'
P. A., 233.

Fled' like/ a glit'ter/ing riv'/ulet/ to the tarn'
L. E., 52.

Hear'est/ thou' this'/ great' voice'/ that shakes'/ the world,'
P. A., 139.

Clang' bat'/tle-axe/ and clash'/ brand!' / Let the/ King' reign.'
C. A., 492.

REFERENCES

Hallam Tennyson: *Alfred Lord Tennyson: A Memoir.*
Henry Van Dyke: *The Poetry of Tennyson.*
Stopford Brooke: *Tennyson, His Art and Relation to Modern Life.*
Edward Campbell Tainsh: *A Study of the Works of Tennyson.*
Richard Jones: *The Growth of the Idylls of the King.*
Condé Benoist Pallen: *The Meaning of the Idylls of the King.*
M. W. MacCallum: *Tennyson's Idylls of the King.*
Sir Edward Strachey: *Malory's Morte D'arthur*, Globe Edition.

TEACHING THE IDYLLS OF THE KING

The Idylls in the High School. In the entire range of our rich and varied literature there is nothing better fitted to serve the purposes of literary study in the high school than Tennyson's *Idylls of the King*. The youthful love of heroism and romance finds kindred spirits in Gareth and Lynette; the awakening ethical sense recognizes ideals of surpassing elevation and purity in Arthur and Elaine; and the growing consciousness of the never-ceasing warfare between right and wrong sympathizes with the soul-struggle of Lancelot and the beautiful Queen. The rapturous music of our mightiest lyrist commands ready response in the quick, joyous ear of youth, and the inspirational power of an intensely human story told in almost faultless verse contributes to the slow, unconscious process of cultivating literary appreciation.

"Guinevere" Necessary. If the story is to be told so as to bring out its full ethical and spiritual content, the Idyll "Guinevere" must be studied. Without it, not only is the plot incomplete, but also the treatment of the theme is lacking in its deepest import and its most profound spiritual truth. Nowhere else in the Idylls is there more enchanting music or more penetrating insight into human life and character. It is the keystone of the plot, and the climax of the theme.

The Theme of the Idylls. In "Gareth and Lynette" Tennyson hints that the theme is

"The war of Time against the soul of man."

Again in the "Epilogue to the Queen" he says,

"accept this old imperfect tale,
New-old, and shadowing Sense at war with Soul."

15

Elsewhere the poet said, "The whole is a dream of a man coming into practical life and ruined by one sin." The specific form of this warfare is found in the growth of the guilty love between Lancelot and Guinevere, and in its effect upon the structure of the ideal society upon whose perpetuity depended all the projects of the King. In a generalized form it may be said that the theme is the effect upon society of sin in high place. Throughout the study, this theme and its relation to the various poems should be kept in mind. In the notes prefixed to the text on "Lancelot and Elaine," "Gareth and Lynette," and "Guinevere," is discussed briefly the relation of each of these poems to the theme, and the development of the theme in those of the Idylls not included in the present edition. It is greatly to be desired that the pupils may read the entire twelve poems with this development in mind.

The Allegory. In contrast with the theme, which is essential to any intelligent study of the Idylls, stands the allegory, which is generally confusing. In a few instances, such as in the passage describing the Lady of the Lake in "Gareth and Lynette," 210, ff., and the Hermit's cave, 1166, ff., some attention to the allegory is necessary. But any attempt to make the leading characters other than real flesh and blood will in most cases dim the glamor of the poetry into the light of common day. There is unquestionably a moral and spiritual lesson in all great literature, but this lesson must be taught by its portrayal of typical conditions in which the reader recognizes his own real or potential merits and defects, rather than by preachy moralizing.

Aims of Studying the Idylls. It is coming to be generally recognized that the study of literature has a much higher aim than to impart mere information. Less and less attention is being paid to details of the author's life, sources of the plot, obscure allusions, and rhetorical classifications. Study of the literature itself for the development of a discriminating appreciation of the best books has taken the place of abstruse lectures and voluminous commentaries. Like other elements of our modern curriculum, literature is taking its place as a vital force in shaping the lives of our youth.

Proper study of such literature as the Idylls should lessen the number of young people who pass through the great awakening period of adolescence without apparently seeing any of the deeper problems of life, or coming to a fuller appreciation of their own personality and its responsibilities. If, in addition to this, these masterpieces are to contribute anything to the real education of the boys and girls studying them, that contribution will consist in the attitude toward similar literature that comes from what Professor Hiram Corson terms "the assimilation of the informing life of these works of genius." This is a slow process, like the mysterious city of Camelot,

> "built
> To music, therefore never built at all,
> And therefore built forever."

In his charming little volume, *The Aims of Literary Study,* Professor Corson says: "Literature is not a mere knowledge subject as the word *knowledge* is usually understood, namely, that with which the discursive, formulating intellect has to do. But it *is* a knowledge subject (only that and nothing more) if that higher form of knowledge be meant, which is quite outside of the domain of the intellect—a knowledge which is a matter of spiritual consciousness and which the intellect cannot translate into judgment."

It follows, then, that the excellence of the instruction in these poems must depend largely upon the teacher's absorption of their music and of their spiritual truth, and upon her inspirational power to arouse a ready response to these essential elements.

Methods. Probably the most valuable single element in teaching these poems is the sympathetic reading of the teacher. Her interpretation will be a model for the pupils' reading and it will illumine the fine passages as they can be illumined by no amount of discussion. Discussion may interpret the thought, but the oral reading will bring a response to that subtle union of sound, sense, and emotion that is so large an element in poetry. She should encourage the pupils to read aloud at home in preparing their lessons, and she should test the thoroughness of this preparation by the sympathy and power of their oral reading in class. Written examinations will to some extent test the amount of external knowledge a pupil may have of a poem, but they will never test his absorption of its "informing life" as will his oral interpretation.

The oral reading will furnish pupils with an answer to one question that should be a part of each day's recitation, "What are the fine lines in to-day's lesson?" These lines should be marked, and a large number of those which particularly appeal to each individual should be memorized, in addition to a few of the finest passages prescribed by the teacher.

The method of memorizing is quite as important as the fact. If pupils will read aloud the passages selected, once or twice a day for a couple of weeks, they will find that they have unconsciously mastered them. Moreover, the passages so memorized will have become a permanent possession; while if they are learned in shorter sections in a single day, they will be retained little later than the examination. The reason for this is obvious. Not only does the ear as well as the eye help to make the impression permanent, but more important still, the muscular memory is enlisted for the same end in the form of reflex action of the vocal organs. When the passages that particularly appeal to the pupil have been memorized in this way, the process of absorption and of appreciative literary culture has been begun.

The notes at the back of the book are given in the hope that they may contribute to the understanding of necessary details and that they may suggest helpful lines of discussion. Among these notes are frequent questions on syntax. These are given only where the answer will be of value in making the meaning clear,—never for merely grammatical purposes. All of this material, however, need occupy very little of the class time. An occasional written test of ten minutes, given without previous warning, will be likely to insure the mastery of these details, and will leave the valuable class-time free for reading and for discussion of the real teaching points in the literature. Throughout the notes there are suggestive questions that emphasize the most important topics dealing with human life and character. The study of these questions, as well as of those arising in class, will encourage pupils to make their own individual comments, and will thus call out much spontaneity and originality.

There is great danger that exhaustive attention to voluminous notes may emphasize the wrong motive for study of literature, particularly of poetry, where the real value is in the spirit rather than the letter. Worse even than excessive study of notes is the practice, now happily disappearing, of reproducing the story as part of the theme work of the class. This is specially unfortunate in the study of the higher type of poetry. A glorious tale told in glorious verse becomes as bald and prosaic as the solution of a problem in algebra when reproduced in the stilted, commonplace English of a high school composition. This treatment of such poetry as *The Idylls of the King* destroys "the consecration and the poet's dream" that the child has a right to realize.

Perhaps the most difficult as well as the most essential task for the young teacher of English fresh from college or university training is to leave the ideals of the seminar and get the point of view of the high school student. For our boys and girls, critical study is undesirable as well as impossible. For the teacher, it is highly desirable if viewed in its right perspective. It would be fortunate for both teachers and pupils if they could apply the principles stated in the following passage from Littledale's *Essays on Lord Tennyson's Idylls of the King:*

"Critical study of an author is very well in its way, and useful as a preparation for the appreciation of a poem. But it is only truly useful in the sense that a study of the sciences helps our appreciation of the works of the Creator. Such learning is a means and not the end. We must look at nature with direct eyes, and not through the medium of books, if we would commune with the spirit of nature; and we must read poetry, not for the sake of the particles of literary dust that adhere to it, but for its own sake, and for the poet's sake, sincerely and sympathetically. Only by doing so can we really bring our own small hearts into contact with the large heart of the poet. Only thus can a great poem like *The Idylls of the King* become to us 'the precious life-blood of a master spirit, embalmed and treasured up on purpose to a life beyond life.'"

The teacher must often feel that it is a hopeless task in any adequate way to interpret the matchless beauty of these poems. Only by long and loving companionship can there be a full response to their harmonies. Only in a classroom attuned to the sweeter music of the spirit can the teacher help along the process of absorption. Even then she will be painfully conscious of the fact that there is no human means of measuring the results of her efforts. If her work bears fruit in a deeper resourcefulness of spirit, in a readier response to truth and beauty, it will not have been done in vain.

THE ORDER OF THE IDYLLS OF THE KING

The Coming of Arthur
Gareth and Lynette
The Marriage of Geraint
Geraint and Enid
Balin and Balan
Merlin and Vivien
Lancelot and Elaine
The Holy Grail
Pelleas and Ettarre
The Last Tournament
Guinevere
The Passing of Arthur

IDYLLS OF THE KING

IDYLLS OF THE KING

THE COMING OF ARTHUR

The first of the Idylls, "The Coming of Arthur," is founded on Malory's *Morte Darthur*, but like all of the poems it varies widely from the original. It deals with the birth of the King, the establishment of his rule, his war with the revolting petty kings who question his right to the throne, his marriage with Guinevere, and the establishment of the Order of the Table Round.

LEODOGRAN, the king of Cameliard,
Had one fair daughter, and none other child;
And she was fairest of all flesh on earth,
Guinevere, and in her his one delight.

For many a petty king ere Arthur came   5
Ruled in this isle and, ever waging war
Each upon other, wasted all the land;
And still from time to time the heathen host
Swarm'd over-seas, and harried what was left.
And so there grew great tracts of wilderness,   10
Wherein the beast was ever more and more,
But man was less and less, till Arthur came.
For first Aurelius lived and fought and died,
And after him King Uther fought and died,

But either fail'd to make the kingdom one.   15
And after these King Arthur for a space,
And thro' the puissance of his Table Round,
Drew all their petty princedoms under him,
Their king and head, and made a realm and reign'd.

And thus the land of Cameliard was waste,   20
Thick with wet woods, and many a beast therein,
And none or few to scare or chase the beast;
So that wild dog and wolf and boar and bear
Came night and day, and rooted in the fields,
And wallow'd in the gardens of the King.   25
And ever and anon the wolf would steal
The children and devour, but now and then,
Her own brood lost or dead, lent her fierce teat
To human sucklings; and the children, housed
In her foul den, there at their meat would growl,   30
And mock their foster-mother on four feet,
Till, straighten'd, they grew up to wolf-like men,
Worse than the wolves. And King Leodogran
Groan'd for the Roman legions here again
And Cæsar's eagle: then his brother king,   35
Urien, assail'd him: last a heathen horde,
Reddening the sun with smoke and earth with blood,
And on the spike that split the mother's heart
Spitting the child, brake on him, till, amazed,
He knew not whither he should turn for aid.   40

But—for he heard of Arthur newly crown'd,
Tho' not without an uproar made by those

Who cried, "He is not Uther's son"—the King
Sent to him, saying, "Arise, and help us thou!
For here between the man and beast we die."   45

And Arthur yet had done no deed of arms,
But heard the call and came: and Guinevere
Stood by the castle walls to watch him pass;
But since he neither wore on helm or shield
The golden symbol of his kinglihood,   50
But rode a simple knight among his knights,
And many of these in richer arms than he,
She saw him not, or mark'd not, if she saw,
One among many, tho' his face was bare.
But Arthur, looking downward as he past,   55
Felt the light of her eyes into his life
Smite on the sudden, yet rode on, and pitch'd
His tents beside the forest. Then he drave
The heathen; after, slew the beast, and fell'd
The forest, letting in the sun, and made   60
Broad pathways for the hunter and the knight,
And so return'd.

         For while he linger'd there,
A doubt that ever smoulder'd in the hearts
Of those great lords and barons of his realm
Flash'd forth and into war; for most of these,   65
Colleaguing with a score of petty kings,
Made head against him, crying: "Who is he
That he should rule us? who hath proven him
King Uther's son? for lo! we look at him,

And find nor face nor bearing, limbs nor voice,   70
Are like to those of Uther whom we knew.
This is the son of Gorloïs, not the King;
This is the son of Anton, not the King."

And Arthur, passing thence to battle, felt
Travail, and throes and agonies of the life,   75
Desiring to be join'd with Guinevere,
And thinking as he rode: "Her father said
That there between the man and beast they die.
Shall I not lift her from this land of beasts
Up to my throne and side by side with me?   80
What happiness to reign a lonely king,
Vext—O ye stars that shudder over me,
O earth that soundest hollow under me,
Vext with waste dreams? for saving I be join'd
To her that is the fairest under heaven,   85
I seem as nothing in the mighty world,
And cannot will my will nor work my work
Wholly, nor make myself in mine own realm
Victor and lord. But were I join'd with her,
Then might we live together as one life,   90
And reigning with one will in everything
Have power on this dark land to lighten it,
And power on this dead world to make it live."

Thereafter—as he speaks who tells the tale—
When Arthur reach'd a field of battle bright   95
With pitch'd pavilions of his foe, the world
Was all so clear about him that he saw

The smallest rock far on the faintest hill,
And even in high day the morning star.
So when the King had set his banner broad, 100
At once from either side, with trumpet-blast,
And shouts, and clarions shrilling unto blood,
The long-lanced battle let their horses run.
And now the barons and the kings prevail'd,
And now the King, as here and there that war 105
Went swaying; but the Powers who walk the world
Made lightnings and great thunders over him,
And dazed all eyes, till Arthur by main might,
And mightier of his hands with every blow,
And leading all his knighthood threw the kings 110
Carádos, Urien, Cradlemont of Wales,
Claudius, and Clariance of Northumberland,
The King Brandagoras of Latangor,
With Anguisant of Erin, Morganore,
And Lot of Orkney. Then, before a voice 115
As dreadful as the shout of one who sees
To one who sins, and deems himself alone
And all the world asleep, they swerved and brake
Flying, and Arthur call'd to stay the brands
That hack'd among the flyers, "Ho! they yield!" 120
So like a painted battle the war stood
Silenced, the living quiet as the dead,
And in the heart of Arthur joy was lord.
He laugh'd upon his warrior whom he loved
And honor'd most. "Thou dost not doubt me King,
So well thine arm hath wrought for me to-day." 126
"Sir and my liege," he cried, "the fire of God

Descends upon thee in the battle-field:
I know thee for my King!" Whereat the two,
For each had warded either in the fight,   130
Sware on the field of death a deathless love.
And Arthur said, "Man's word is God in man:
Let chance what will, I trust thee to the death."

Then quickly from the foughten field he sent
Ulfius, and Brastias, and Bedivere,   135
His new-made knights, to King Leodogran,
Saying, "If I in aught have served thee well,
Give me thy daughter Guinevere to wife."

Whom when he heard, Leodogran in heart
Debating—"How should I that am a king,   140
However much he holp me at my need,
Give my one daughter saving to a king,
And a king's son?"—lifted his voice, and call'd
A hoary man, his chamberlain, to whom
He trusted all things, and of him required   145
His counsel: "Knowest thou aught of Arthur's birth?"

Then spake the hoary chamberlain and said:
"Sir King, there be but two old men that know;
And each is twice as old as I: and one
Is Merlin, the wise man that ever served   150
King Uther thro' his magic art; and one
Is Merlin's master—so they call him—Bleys,
Who taught him magic; but the scholar ran
Before the master, and so far that Bleys

Laid magic by, and sat him down, and wrote   155
All things and whatsoever Merlin did
In one great annal-book, where after-years
Will learn the secret of our Arthur's birth."

To whom the King Leodogran replied:
"O friend, had I been holpen half as well   160
By this King Arthur as by thee to-day,
Then beast and man had had their share of me;
But summon here before us yet once more
Ulfius, and Brastias, and Bedivere."

Then, when they came before him, the King said: 165
"I have seen the cuckoo chased by lesser fowl,
And reason in the chase; but wherefore now
Do these your lords stir up the heat of war,
Some calling Arthur born of Gorloïs,
Others of Anton? Tell me, ye yourselves,   170
Hold ye this Arthur for King Uther's son?"

And Ulfius and Brastias answer'd, "Ay."
Then Bedivere, the first of all his knights
Knighted by Arthur at his crowning, spake—
For bold in heart and act and word was he,   175
Whenever slander breathed against the King—

"Sir, there be many rumors on this head:
For there be those who hate him in their hearts,
Call him baseborn, and since his ways are sweet,
And theirs are bestial, hold him less than man;   180

And there be those who deem him more than man,
And dream he dropt from heaven: but my belief
In all this matter—so ye care to learn—
Sir, for ye know that in King Uther's time
The prince and warrior Gorloïs, he that held   185
Tintagil castle by the Cornish sea,
Was wedded with a winsome wife, Ygerne;
And daughters had she borne him,—one whereof,
Lot's wife, the Queen of Orkney, Bellicent,
Hath ever like a loyal sister cleaved   190
To Arthur,—but a son she had not borne.
And Uther cast upon her eyes of love;
But she, a stainless wife to Gorloïs,
So loathed the bright dishonor of his love
That Gorloïs and King Uther went to war,   195
And overthrown was Gorloïs and slain.
Then Uther in his wrath and heat besieged
Ygerne within Tintagil, where her men,
Seeing the mighty swarm about their walls,
Left her and fled, and Uther enter'd in,   200
And there was none to call to but himself.
So, compass'd by the power of the King,
Enforced she was to wed him in her tears,
And with a shameful swiftness; afterward,
Not many moons, King Uther died himself,   205
Moaning and wailing for an heir to rule
After him, lest the realm should go to wrack.
And that same night, the night of the new year,
By reason of the bitterness and grief
That vext his mother, all before his time   **210**

Was Arthur born, and all as soon as born
Deliver'd at a secret postern-gate
To Merlin, to be holden far apart
Until his hour should come; because the lords
Of that fierce day were as the lords of this,   215
Wild beasts, and surely would have torn the child
Piecemeal among them, had they known; for each
But sought to rule for his own self and hand,
And many hated Uther for the sake
Of Gorloïs.   Wherefore Merlin took the child,   220
And gave him to Sir Anton, an old knight
And ancient friend of Uther; and his wife
Nursed the young prince, and rear'd him with her own;
And no man knew.   And ever since the lords
Have foughten like wild beasts among themselves,   225
So that the realm has gone to wrack; but now,
This year, when Merlin—for his hour had come—
Brought Arthur forth, and set him in the hall,
Proclaiming, 'Here is Uther's heir, your king,'
A hundred voices cried: 'Away with him!   230
No king of ours! a son of Gorloïs he;
Or else the child of Anton, and no king,
Or else baseborn.'   Yet Merlin thro' his craft,
And while the people clamor'd for a king,
Had Arthur crown'd; but after, the great lords   235
Banded, and so brake out in open war."

Then while the King debated with himself
If Arthur were the child of shamefulness,
Or born the son of Gorloïs after death,

Or Uther's son and born before his time,   240
Or whether there were truth in anything
Said by these three, there came to Cameliard,
With Gawain and young Modred, her two sons,
Lot's wife, the Queen of Orkney, Bellicent;
Whom as he could, not as he would, the King   245
Made feast for, saying, as they sat at meat:
"A doubtful throne is ice on summer seas.
Ye come from Arthur's court.   Victor his men
Report him!   Yea, but ye—think ye this king—
So many those that hate him, and so strong,   250
So few his knights, however brave they be—
Hath body enow to hold his foemen down?"

    "O King," she cried, "and I will tell thee: few,
Few, but all brave, all of one mind with him;
For I was near him when the savage yells   255
Of Uther's peerage died, and Arthur sat
Crowned on the daïs, and his warriors cried,
'Be thou the king, and we will work thy will
Who love thee.'   Then the King in low deep tones,
And simple words of great authority,   260
Bound them by so strait vows to his own self
That when they rose, knighted from kneeling, some
Were pale as at the passing of a ghost,
Some flush'd, and others dazed, as one who wakes
Half-blinded at the coming of a light.   265

    "But when he spake, and cheer'd his Table Round
With large, divine, and comfortable words,

Beyond my tongue to tell thee—I beheld
From eye to eye thro' all their Order flash
A momentary likeness of the King;   270
And ere it left their faces, thro' the cross
And those around it and the Crucified,
Down from the casement over Arthur, smote
Flame-color, vert, and azure, in three rays,
One falling upon each of three fair queens   275
Who stood in silence near his throne, the friends
Of Arthur, gazing on him, tall, with bright
Sweet faces, who will help him at his need.

"And there I saw mage Merlin, whose vast wit
And hundred winters are but as the hands   280
Of loyal vassals toiling for their liege.

"And near him stood the Lady of the Lake,
Who knows a subtler magic than his own—
Clothed in white samite, mystic, wonderful.
She gave the King his huge cross-hilted sword,   285
Whereby to drive the heathen out: a mist
Of incense curl'd about her, and her face
Wellnigh was hidden in the minster gloom;
But there was heard among the holy hymns
A voice as of the waters, for she dwells   290
Down in a deep—calm, whatsoever storms
May shake the world—and when the surface rolls,
Hath power to walk the waters like our Lord.

"There likewise I beheld Excalibur
Before him at his crowning borne, the sword   295

That rose from out the bosom of the lake,
And Arthur row'd across and took it—rich
With jewels, elfin Urim, on the hilt,
Bewildering heart and eye—the blade so bright
That men are blinded by it—on one side,   300
Graven in the oldest tongue of all this world,
'Take me,' but turn the blade and ye shall see,
And written in the speech ye speak yourself,
'Cast me away!' And sad was Arthur's face
Taking it, but old Merlin counsell'd him,   305
'Take thou and strike! the time to cast away
Is yet far-off.' So this great brand the king
Took, and by this will beat his foemen down."

Thereat Leodogran rejoiced, but thought
To sift his doubtings to the last, and ask'd,   310
Fixing full eyes of question on her face,
"The swallow and the swift are near akin,
But thou art closer to this noble prince,
Being his own dear sister"; and she said,
"Daughter of Gorloïs and Ygerne am I";   315
"And therefore Arthur's sister?" ask'd the King.
She answer'd, "These be secret things," and sign'd
To those two sons to pass, and let them be.
And Gawain went, and breaking into song
Sprang out, and follow'd by his flying hair   320
Ran like a colt, and leapt at all he saw;
But Modred laid his ear beside the doors,
And there half-heard—the same that afterward
Struck for the throne, and striking found his doom.

And then the Queen made answer: "What know I?
For dark my mother was in eyes and hair,   326
And dark in hair and eyes am I; and dark
Was Gorloïs; yea, and dark was Uther too,
Wellnigh to blackness; but this king is fair
Beyond the race of Britons and of men.   330
Moreover, always in my mind I hear
A cry from out the dawning of my life,
A mother weeping, and I hear her say,
'O that ye had some brother, pretty one,
To guard thee on the rough ways of the world.'"   335

"Ay," said the King, "and hear ye such a cry?
But when did Arthur chance upon thee first?"

"O King!" she cried, "and I will tell thee true:
He found me first when yet a little maid:
Beaten I had been for a little fault   340
Whereof I was not guilty; and out I ran
And flung myself down on a bank of heath,
And hated this fair world and all therein,
And wept, and wish'd that I were dead; and he—
I know not whether of himself he came,   345
Or brought by Merlin, who, they say, can walk
Unseen at pleasure—he was at my side,
And spake sweet words, and comforted my heart,
And dried my tears, being a child with me.
And many a time he came, and evermore   350
As I grew greater grew with me; and sad
At times he seem'd, and sad with him was I,

Stern too at times, and then I loved him not,
But sweet again, and then I loved him well.
And now of late I see him less and less,　　　　355
But those first days had golden hours for me,
For then I surely thought he would be king.

"But let me tell thee now another tale:
For Bleys, our Merlin's master, as they say,
Died but of late, and sent his cry to me,　　　　360
To hear him speak before he left his life.
Shrunk like a fairy changeling lay the mage;
And when I enter'd told me that himself
And Merlin ever served about the King,
Uther, before he died; and on the night　　　　365
When Uther in Tintagil past away
Moaning and wailing for an heir, the two
Left the still King, and passing forth to breathe,
Then from the castle gateway by the chasm
Descending thro' the dismal night—a night　　　　370
in which the bounds of heaven and earth were
　　　lost—
Beheld, so high upon the dreary deeps
It seem'd in heaven, a ship, the shape thereof
A dragon wing'd, and all from stem to stern
Bright with a shining people on the decks,　　　　375
And gone as soon as seen.　And then the two
Dropt to the cove, and watch'd the great sea fall,
Wave after wave, each mightier than the last,
Till last, a ninth one, gathering half the deep
And full of voices, slowly rose and plunged　　　　380

Roaring, and all the wave was in a flame:
And down the wave and in the flame was borne
A naked babe, and rode to Merlin's feet,
Who stoopt and caught the babe, and cried, 'The
      King!
Here is an heir for Uther!' And the fringe   385
Of that great breaker, sweeping up the strand,
Lash'd at the wizard as he spake the word,
And all at once all round him rose in fire,
So that the child and he were clothed in fire.
And presently thereafter follow'd calm,   390
Free sky and stars: 'And this same child,' he said,
'Is he who reigns; nor could I part in peace
Till this were told.' And saying this the seer
Went thro' the strait and dreadful pass of death,
Not ever to be question'd any more   395
Save on the further side; but when I met
Merlin, and ask'd him if these things were truth—
The shining dragon and the naked child
Descending in the glory of the seas—
He laugh'd as is his wont, and answer'd me   400
In riddling triplets of old time, and said:—

"'Rain, rain, and sun! a rainbow in the sky!
A young man will be wiser by and by;
An old man's wit may wander ere he die.

"'Rain, rain, and sun! a rainbow on the lea!   405
And truth is this to me, and that to thee;
And truth or clothed or naked let it be.

"'Rain, sun, and rain! and the free blossom blows:
Sun, rain, and sun! and where is he who knows?
From the great deep to the great deep he goes.'"   410

"So Merlin riddling anger'd me; but thou
Fear not to give this King thine only child,
Guinevere: so great bards of him will sing
Hereafter; and dark sayings from of old
Ranging and ringing thro' the minds of men,   415
And echo'd by old folk beside their fires
For comfort after their wage-work is done,
Speak of the King; and Merlin in our time
Hath spoken also, not in jest, and sworn
Tho' men may wound him that he will not die,   420
But pass, again to come, and then or now
Utterly smite the heathen underfoot,
Till these and all men hail him for their king."

She spake and King Leodogran rejoiced,
But musing "Shall I answer yea or nay?"   425
Doubted, and drowsed, nodded and slept, and saw,
Dreaming, a slope of land that ever grew,
Field after field, up to a height, the peak
Haze-hidden and thereon a phantom king,
Now looming, and now lost; and on the slope   430
The sword rose, the hind fell, the herd was driven,
Fire glimpsed; and all the land from roof and rick,
In drifts of smoke before a rolling wind,
Stream'd to the peak, and mingled with the haze
And made it thicker; while the phantom king   435

Sent out at times a voice; and here or there
Stood one who pointed toward the voice, the rest
Slew on and burnt, crying, "No king of ours,
No son of Uther, and no king of ours;"
Till with a wink his dream was changed, the haze   440
Descended, and the solid earth became
As nothing, but the King stood out in heaven,
Crown'd. And Leodogran awoke, and sent
Ulfius, and Brastias, and Bedivere,
Back to the court of Arthur answering yea.   445

Then Arthur charged his warrior whom he loved
And honor'd most, Sir Lancelot, to ride forth
And bring the Queen, and watch'd him from the gates;
And Lancelot past away among the flowers—
For then was latter April—and return'd   450
Among the flowers, in May, with Guinevere.
To whom arrived, by Dubric the high saint,
Chief of the church in Britain, and before
The stateliest of her altar-shrines, the King
That morn was married, while in stainless white,   455
The fair beginners of a nobler time,
And glorying in their vows and him, his knights
Stood round him, and rejoicing in his joy.
Far shone the fields of May thro' open door,
The sacred altar blossom'd white with May,   460
The Sun of May descended on their King,
They gazed on all earth's beauty in their Queen,
Roll'd incense, and there past along the hymns
A voice as of the waters, while the two

Sware at the shrine of Christ a deathless love: 465
And Arthur said, "Behold, thy doom is mine.
Let chance what will, I love thee to the death!"
To whom the Queen replied with drooping eyes,
"King and my lord, I love thee to the death!"
And holy Dubric spread his hands and spake: 470
"Reign ye, and live and love, and make the world
Other, and may thy Queen be one with thee,
And all this Order of thy Table Round
Fulfil the boundless purpose of their King!"

So Dubric said; but when they left the shrine   475
Great lords from Rome before the portal stood,
In scornful stillness gazing as they past;
Then while they paced a city all on fire
With sun and cloth of gold, the trumpets blew,
And Arthur's knighthood sang before the King:—   480

"Blow trumpet, for the world is white with May!
Blow trumpet, the long night hath roll'd away!
Blow thro' the living world—'Let the King reign!'

"Shall Rome or Heathen rule in Arthur's realm?
Flash brand and lance, fall battle-axe upon helm,   485
Fall battle-axe, and flash brand! Let the King reign!

"Strike for the King and live! his knights have
    heard
That God hath told the King a secret word.
Fall battle-axe, and flash brand! Let the King reign!

"Blow trumpet! he will lift us from the dust.   490
Blow trumpet! live the strength, and die the lust!
Clang battle-axe, and clash brand! Let the King
    reign!

"Strike for the King and die! and if thou diest,
The King is king, and ever wills the highest.
Clang battle-axe, and clash brand! Let the King
    reign!   495

"Blow, for our Sun is mighty in his May!
Blow, for our Sun is mightier day by day!
Clang battle-axe, and clash brand! Let the King
    reign!

"The King will follow Christ, and we the King,
In whom high God hath breathed a secret thing.   500
Fall battle-axe, and clash brand! Let the King
    reign!"

So sang the knighthood, moving to their hall.
There at the banquet those great lords from Rome,
The slowly-fading mistress of the world,
Strode in and claim'd their tribute as of yore.   505
But Arthur spake: "Behold, for these have sworn
To wage my wars, and worship me their King;
The old order changeth, yielding place to new;
And we that fight for our fair father Christ,
Seeing that ye be grown too weak and old   510
To drive the heathen from your Roman wall,

No tribute will we pay." So those great lords
Drew back in wrath, and Arthur strove with Rome.

And Arthur and his knighthood for a space
Were all one will, and thro' that strength the King 515
Drew in the petty princedoms under him,
Fought, and in twelve great battles overcame
The heathen hordes, and made a realm and reign'd.

GARETH AND LYNETTE

"Gareth and Lynette" shows the kingdom at its best, before the sin of Lancelot and the Queen has begun its deadly work. Gareth is a noble youth, who finds in the pure life of the court the conditions most favorable to the realization of his ambition to do a man's work for Christ and the King.

THE last tall son of Lot and Bellicent,
And tallest, Gareth, in a showerful spring
Stared at the spate. A slender-shafted pine
Lost footing, fell, and so was whirl'd away.
"How he went down," said Gareth, "as a false knight
Or evil king before my lance, if lance   6
Were mine to use—O senseless cataract,
Bearing all down in thy precipitancy—
And yet thou art but swollen with cold snows
And mine is living blood: thou dost His will,   10
The Maker's, and not knowest, and I that know
Have strength and wit, in my good mother's hal
Linger with vacillating obedience,
Prison'd, and kept and coax'd and whistled to—
Since the good mother holds me still a child!   1ͨ
Good mother is bad mother unto me!
A worse were better; yet no worse would I.
Heaven yield her for it, but in me put force
To weary her ears with one continuous prayer,

Until she let me fly discaged to sweep   20
In ever-highering eagle-circles up
To the great Sun of Glory, and thence swoop
Down upon all things base, and dash them dead,
A knight of Arthur, working out his will,
To cleanse the world. Why, Gawain, when he came 25
With Modred hither in the summer-time,
Ask'd me to tilt with him, the proven knight.
Modred for want of worthier was the judge.
Then I so shook him in the saddle, he said,
'Thou hast half prevail'd against me,' said so—he—   30
Tho' Modred biting his thin lips was mute,
For he is alway sullen: what care I?"

   And Gareth went, and hovering round her chair
Ask'd, "Mother, tho' ye count me still the child,
Sweet mother, do ye love the child?" She laugh'd, 35
"Thou art but a wild-goose to question it."
"Then, mother, an ye love the child," he said,
"Being a goose and rather tame than wild,
Hear the child's story." "Yea, my well-beloved,
An 'twere but of the goose and golden eggs."   40

   And Gareth answer'd her with kindling eyes:
"Nay, nay, good mother, but this egg of mine
Was finer gold than any goose can lay;
For this an eagle, a royal eagle, laid
Almost beyond eye-reach, on such a palm   45
As glitters gilded in thy Book of Hours.
And there was ever haunting round the palm

A lusty youth, but poor, who often saw
The splendor sparkling from aloft, and thought,
'An I could climb and lay my hand upon it, 50
Then were I wealthier than a leash of kings.'
But ever when he reach'd a hand to climb,
One that had loved him from his childhood caught
And stay'd him, 'Climb not lest thou break thy neck,
I charge thee by my love,' and so the boy, 55
Sweet mother, neither clomb nor brake his neck,
But brake his very heart in pining for it,
And past away."

    To whom the mother said,
"True love, sweet son, had risk'd himself and climb'd,
And handed down the golden treasure to him." 60

And Gareth answer'd her with kindling eyes:
"Gold? said I gold?—ay then, why he, or she,
Or whoseso'er it was, or half the world
Had ventured—*had* the thing I spake of been
Mere gold—but this was all of that true steel 65
Whereof they forged the brand Excalibur,
And lightnings play'd about it in the storm,
And all the little fowl were flurried at it,
And there were cries and clashings in the nest,
That sent him from his senses: let me go." 70

Then Bellicent bemoan'd herself and said:
"Hast thou no pity upon my loneliness?
Lo, where thy father Lot beside the hearth

Lies like a log, and all but smoulder'd out!
For ever since when traitor to the King 75
He fought against him in the barons' war,
And Arthur gave him back his territory,
His age hath slowly droopt, and now lies there
A yet-warm corpse, and yet unburiable,
No more; nor sees, nor hears, nor speaks, nor knows. 80
And both thy brethren are in Arthur's hall,
Albeit neither loved with that full love
I feel for thee, nor worthy such a love.
Stay therefore thou; red berries charm the bird,
And thee, mine innocent, the jousts, the wars, 85
Who never knewest finger-ache, nor pang
Of wrench'd or broken limb—an often chance
In those brain-stunning shocks, and tourney-falls,
Frights to my heart; but stay: follow the deer
By these tall firs and our fast-falling burns; 90
So make thy manhood mightier day by day;
Sweet is the chase: and I will seek thee out
Some comfortable bride and fair, to grace
Thy climbing life, and cherish my prone year,
Till falling into Lot's forgetfulness 95
I know not thee, myself, nor anything.
Stay, my best son! ye are yet more boy than man."

Then Gareth: "An ye hold me yet for child,
Hear yet once more the story of the child.
For, mother, there was once a king, like ours. 100
The prince his heir, when tall and marriageable,
Ask'd for a bride; and thereupon the king

Set two before him. One was fair, strong, **arm'd**—
But to be won by force—and many men
Desired her; one, good lack, no man desired.   105
And these were the conditions of the king:
That save he won the first by force, he needs
Must wed that other, whom no man desired,
A red-faced bride who knew herself so vile
That evermore she long'd to hide herself,   110
Nor fronted man or woman, eye to eye—
Yea—some she cleaved to, but they died of her.
And one—they call'd her Fame; and one—O mother,
How can ye keep me tether'd to you?—Shame.
Man am I grown, a man's work must I do.   115
Follow the deer? follow the Christ, the King,
Live pure, speak true, right wrong, follow the
        King—
Else, wherefore born?"

                To whom the mother said:
"Sweet son, for there be many who deem him not,
Or will not deem him, wholly proven King—   120
Albeit in mine own heart I knew him King
When I was frequent with him in my youth,
And heard him kingly speak, and doubted him
No more than he, himself; but felt him mine,
Of closest kin to me: yet—wilt thou leave   125
Thine easeful biding here, and risk thine all,
Life, limbs, for one that is not proven King?
Stay, till the cloud that settles round his birth
Hath lifted but a little. Stay, sweet son."

And Gareth answer'd quickly: "Not an hour,   130
So that ye yield me—I will walk thro' fire,
Mother, to gain it—your full leave to go.
Not proven, who swept the dust of ruin'd Rome
From off the threshold of the realm, and crush'd
The idolaters, and made the people free?   135
Who should be king save him who makes us free?"

So when the Queen, who long had sought in
        vain
To break him from the intent to which he grew,
Found her son's will unwaveringly one,
She answer'd craftily: "Will ye walk thro' fire?   140
Who walks thro' fire will hardly heed the smoke.
Ay, go then, an ye must: only one proof,
Before thou ask the King to make thee knight,
Of thine obedience and thy love to me,
Thy mother,—I demand."

                        And Gareth cried: 145
"A hard one, or a hundred, so I go.
Nay—quick! the proof to prove me to the quick!"

But slowly spake the mother looking at him:
"Prince, thou shalt go disguised to Arthur's hall,
And hire thyself to serve for meats and drinks   150
Among the scullions and the kitchen-knaves,
And those that hand the dish across the bar.
Nor shalt thou tell thy name to any one.
And thou shalt serve a twelvemonth and a day."

For so the Queen believed that when her son   155
Beheld his only way to glory lead
Low down thro' villain kitchen-vassalage,
Her own true Gareth was too princely-proud
To pass thereby; so should he rest with her,
Closed in her castle from the sound of arms.   160

Silent awhile was Gareth, then replied:
"The thrall in person may be free in soul,
And I shall see the jousts. Thy son am I,
And, since thou art my mother, must obey.
I therefore yield me freely to thy will;   165
For hence will I, disguised, and hire myself
To serve with scullions and with kitchen-knaves·
Nor tell my name to any—no, not the King."

Gareth awhile linger'd. The mother's eye
Full of the wistful fear that he would go,   170
And turning toward him wheresoe'er he turn'd,
Perplext his outward purpose, till an hour
When, waken'd by the wind which with full voice
Swept bellowing thro' the darkness on to dawn,
He rose, and out of slumber calling two   175
That still had tended on him from his birth,
Before the wakeful mother heard him, went.

The three were clad like tillers of the soil.
Southward they set their faces. The birds made
Melody on branch and melody in mid air.   180
The damp hill-slopes were quicken'd into green,

And the live green had kindled into flowers,
For it was past the time of Easter-day.

So, when their feet were planted on the plain
That broaden'd toward the base of Camelot,   185
Far off they saw the silver-misty morn
Rolling her smoke about the royal mount,
That rose between the forest and the field.
At times the summit of the high city flash'd;
At times the spires and turrets half-way down   190
Prick'd thro' the mist; at times the great gate shone
Only, that open'd on the field below:
Anon, the whole fair city had disappear'd.

Then those who went with Gareth were amazed,
One crying, "Let us go no further, lord: 195
Here is a city of enchanters, built
By fairy kings." The second echo'd him,
"Lord, we have heard from our wise man at home
To northward, that this king is not the King,
But only changeling out of Fairyland,   200
Who drave the heathen hence by sorcery
And Merlin's glamour." Then the first again,
"Lord, there is no such city anywhere,
But all a vision."

                    Gareth answer'd them
With laughter, swearing he had glamour enow   205
In his own blood, his princedom, youth, and hopes,
To plunge old Merlin in the Arabian sea;

o push'd them all unwilling toward the gate.
nd there was no gate like it under heaven.
or barefoot on the keystone, which was lined   210
nd rippled like an ever-fleeting wave,
he Lady of the Lake stood: all her dress
Vept from her sides as water flowing away;
ut like the cross her great and goodly arms
tretch'd under all the cornice and upheld: 215
nd drops of water fell from either hand;
nd down from one a sword was hung, from one
censer, either worn with wind and storm;
nd o'er her breast floated the sacred fish;
nd in the space to left of her, and right,   220
Vere Arthur's wars in weird devices done,
few things and old co-twisted, as if Time
Vere nothing, so inveterately that men
Vere giddy gazing there; and over all
igh on the top were those three queens, the friends
f Arthur, who should help him at his need.   226

Then those with Gareth for so long a space
tared at the figures that at last it seem'd
he dragon-boughts and elvish emblemings
egan to move, seethe, twine, and curl: they call'd 230
o Gareth, "Lord, the gateway is alive."

And Gareth likewise on them fixt his eyes
o long that even to him they seem'd to move.
ut of the city a blast of music peal'd.
ack from the gate started the three, to whom   235

From out thereunder came an ancient man,
Long-bearded, saying, "Who be ye, my sons?"

Then Gareth: "We be tillers of the soil,
Who leaving share in furrow come to see
The glories of our King: but these, my men,—   24
Your city moved so weirdly in the mist—
Doubt if the King be king at all, or come
From Fairyland; and whether this be built
By magic, and by fairy kings and queens;
Or whether there be any city at all,   24
Or all a vision: and this music now
Hath scared them both, but tell thou these the truth."

Then that old Seer made answer, playing on him
And saying: "Son, I have seen the good ship sail
Keel upward, and mast downward, in the heavens,   25
And solid turrets topsy-turvy in air:
And here is truth; but an it please thee not,
Take thou the truth as thou hast told it me.
For truly, as thou sayest, a fairy king
And fairy queens have built the city, son;   25
They came from out a sacred mountain-cleft
Toward the sunrise, each with harp in hand,
And built it to the music of their harps.
And, as thou sayest, it is enchanted, son,
For there is nothing in it as it seems   26
Saving the King; tho' some there be that hold
The King a shadow, and the city real:
Yet take thou heed of him, for, so thou pass

Beneath this archway, then wilt thou become
A thrall to his enchantments, for the King   265
Will bind thee by such vows as is a shame
A man should not be bound by, yet the which
No man can keep; but, so thou dread to swear,
Pass not beneath this gateway, but abide
Without, among the cattle of the field.   270
For an ye heard a music, like enow
They are building still, seeing the city is built
To music, therefore never built at all,
And therefore built for ever."

                   Gareth spake
Anger'd: "Old master, reverence thine own beard   275
That looks as white as utter truth, and seems
Wellnigh as long as thou are statured tall!
Why mockest thou the stranger that hath been
To thee fair-spoken?"

                But the Seer replied:
"Know ye not then the Riddling of the Bards: 280
'Confusion, and illusion, and relation,
Elusion, and occasion, and evasion'?
I mock thee not but as thou mockest me,
And all that see thee, for thou art not who
Thou seemest, but I know thee who thou art.   285
And now thou goest up to mock the King,
Who cannot brook the shadow of any lie."

   Unmockingly the mocker ending here
Turn'd to the right, and past along the plain;

Whom Gareth looking after said: "My men,   29*
Our one white lie sits like a little ghost
Here on the threshold of our enterprise.
Let love be blamed for it, not she, nor I:
Well, we will make amends."

                With all good cheer
He spake and laugh'd, then enter'd with his twain   29*
Camelot, a city of shadowy palaces
And stately, rich in emblem and the work
Of ancient kings who did their days in stone;
Which Merlin's hand, the Mage at Arthur's court,
Knowing all arts, had touch'd, and everywhere,   30*
At Arthur's ordinance, tipt with lessening peak
And pinnacle, and had made it spire to heaven.
And ever and anon a knight would pass
Outward, or inward to the hall: his arms
Clash'd; and the sound was good to Gareth's ear.   30*
And out of bower and casement shyly glanced
Eyes of pure women, wholesome stars of love;
And all about a healthful people stept
As in the presence of a gracious king.

  Then into hall Gareth ascending heard   31*
A voice, the voice of Arthur, and beheld
Far over heads in that long-vaulted hall
The splendor of the presence of the King
Throned, and delivering doom—and look'd 'no more—
But felt his young heart hammering in his ears,   315
And thought, "For this half-shadow of a lie

The truthful King will doom me when I speak."
Yet pressing on, tho' all in fear to find
Sir Gawain or Sir Modred, saw nor one
Nor other, but in all the listening eyes   320
Of those tall knights that ranged about the throne
Clear honor shining like the dewy star
Of dawn, and faith in their great King, with pure
Affection, and the light of victory,
And glory gain'd, and evermore to gain.   325

Then came a widow crying to the King:
"A boon, Sir King! Thy father, Uther, reft
From my dead lord a field with violence;
For howsoe'er at first he proffer'd gold,
Yet, for the field was pleasant in our eyes,   330
We yielded not; and then he reft us of it
Perforce and left us neither gold nor field."

Said Arthur, "Whether would ye? gold or field?"
To whom the woman weeping, "Nay, my lord,
The field was pleasant in my husband's eye."   335

And Arthur: "Have thy pleasant field again,
And thrice the gold for Uther's use thereof,
According to the years. No boon is here,
But justice, so thy say be proven true.
Accursed, who from the wrongs his father did   340
Would shape himself a right!"

                      And while she past,
Came yet another widow crying to him:

"A boon, Sir King!   Thine enemy, King, am I.
With thine own hand thou slewest my dear lord,
A knight of Uther in the barons' war,   345
When Lot and many another rose and fought
Against thee, saying thou wert basely born.
I held with these, and loathe to ask thee aught.
Yet lo! my husband's brother had my son
Thrall'd in his castle, and hath starved him dead,   350
And standeth seized of that inheritance
Which thou that slewest the sire hast left the son.
So, tho' I scarce can ask it thee for hate,
Grant me some knight to do the battle for me,
Kill the foul thief, and wreak me for my son."   355

　　Then strode a good knight forward, crying to him,
"A boon, Sir King!   I am her kinsman, I.
Give me to right her wrong, and slay the man."

　　Then came Sir Kay, the seneschal, and cried,
"A boon, Sir King! even that thou grant her none,   360
This railer, that hath mock'd thee in full hall—
None; or the wholesome boon of gyve and gag."

　　But Arthur: "We sit King, to help the wrong'd
Thro' all our realm.   The woman loves her lord.
Peace to thee, woman, with thy loves and hates!   365
The kings of old had doom'd thee to the flames;
Aurelius Emrys would have scourged thee dead,
And Uther slit thy tongue: but get thee hence—
Lest that rough humor of the kings of old
Return upon me!   Thou that art her kin,   370

Go likewise; lay him low and slay him not,
But bring him here, that I may judge the right,
According to the justice of the King:
Then, be he guilty, by that deathless King
Who lived and died for men, the man shall die."   375

  Then came in hall the messenger of Mark,
A name of evil savor in the land,
The Cornish king. In either hand he bore
What dazzled all, and shone far-off as shines
A field of charlock in the sudden sun   380
Between two showers, a cloth of palest gold,
Which down he laid before the throne, and knelt,
Delivering that his lord, the vassal king,
Was even upon his way to Camelot;
For having heard that Arthur of his grace   385
Had made his goodly cousin Tristram knight,
And, for himself was of the greater state,
Being a king, he trusted his liege-lord
Would yield him this large honor all the more;
So pray'd him well to accept this cloth of gold,   390
In token of true heart and fealty.

  Then Arthur cried to rend the cloth, to rend
In pieces, and so cast it on the hearth.
An oak-tree smoulder'd there. "The goodly knight!
What! shall the shield of Mark stand among these?"
For, midway down the side of that long hall,   396
A stately pile,—whereof along the front,
Some blazon'd, some but carven, and some blank,

There ran a treble range of stony shields,—
Rose, and high-arching overbrow'd the hearth.   400
And under every shield a knight was named.
For this was Arthur's custom in his hall:
When some good knight had done one noble deed,
His arms were carven only; but if twain,
His arms were blazon'd also; but if none,   405
The shield was blank and bare, without a sign
Saving the name beneath: and Gareth saw
The shield of Gawain blazon'd rich and bright,
And Modred's blank as death; and Arthur cried
To rend the cloth and cast it on the hearth.   410

"More like are we to reave him of his crown
Than make him knight because men call him king.
The kings we found, ye know we stay'd their hands
From war among themselves, but left them kings;
Of whom were any bounteous, merciful,   415
Truth-speaking, brave, good livers, them we enroll'd
Among us, and they sit within our hall.
But Mark hath tarnish'd the great name of king,
As Mark would sully the low state of churl;
And, seeing he hath sent us cloth of gold,   420
Return, and meet, and hold him from our eyes,
Lest we should lap him up in cloth of lead,
Silenced for ever—craven—a man of plots,
Craft, poisonous counsels, wayside ambushings—
No fault of thine: let Kay the seneschal   425
Look to thy wants, and send thee satisfied—
Accursed, who strikes nor lets the hand be seen!"

And many another suppliant crying came
With noise of ravage wrought by beast and man,
And evermore a knight would ride away.   430

Last, Gareth leaning both hands heavily
Down on the shoulders of the twain, his men,
Approach'd between them toward the King, and ask'd,
"A boon, Sir King,"—his voice was all ashamed,—
"For see ye not how weak and hunger-worn   435
I seem—leaning on these? grant me to serve
For meat and drink among thy kitchen-knaves
A twelvemonth and a day, nor seek my name.
Hereafter I will fight."

　　　　　　　　To him the King:
"A goodly youth and worth a goodlier boon!   440
But so thou wilt no goodlier, then must Kay,
The master of the meats and drinks, be thine."

He rose and past; then Kay, a man of mien
Wan-sallow as the plant that feels itself
Root-bitten by white lichen:

　　　　　　　　"Lo ye now!   445
This fellow hath broken from some abbey, where,
God wot, he had not beef and brewis enow,
However that might chance! but an he work,
Like any pigeon will I cram his crop,
And sleeker shall he shine than any hog."   450

Then Lancelot standing near: "Sir Seneschal,
Sleuth-hound thou knowest, and gray, and all the hound;

A horse thou knowest, a man thou dost not know:
Broad brows and fair, a fluent hair and fine,
High nose, a nostril large and fine, and hands   455
Large, fair, and fine!—Some young lad's mystery—
But, or from sheepcot or king's hall, the boy
Is noble-natured. Treat him with all grace,
Lest he should come to shame thy judging of him."

    Then Kay: "What murmurest thou of mystery?   460
Think ye this fellow will poison the King's dish?
Nay, for he spake too fool-like: mystery!
Tut, an the lad were noble, he had ask'd
For horse and armor: fair and fine, forsooth!
Sir Fine-face, Sir Fair-hands? but see thou to it   465
That thine own fineness, Lancelot, some fine day
Undo thee not—and leave my man to me."

    So Gareth all for glory underwent
The sooty yoke of kitchen-vassalage,
Ate with young lads his portion by the door,   470
And couch'd at night with grimy kitchen-knaves.
And Lancelot ever spake him pleasantly,
But Kay the seneschal, who lo'ed him not,
Would hustle and harry him, and labor him
Beyond his comrade of the hearth, and set   475
To turn the broach, draw water, or hew wood,
Or grosser tasks; and Gareth bow'd himself
With all obedience to the King, and wrought
All kind of service with a noble ease
That graced the lowliest act in doing it.   480

And when the thralls had talk among themselves,
And one would praise the love that linkt the King
And Lancelot—how the King had saved his life
In battle twice, and Lancelot once the King's—
For Lancelot was first in the tournament,   485
But Arthur mightiest on the battle-field—
Gareth was glad.   Or if some other told
How once the wandering forester at dawn,
Far over the blue tarns and hazy seas,
On Caer-Eryri's highest found the King,   490
A naked babe, of whom the Prophet spake,
"He passes to the Isle Avilion,
He passes and is heal'd and cannot die"—
Gareth was glad.   But if their talk were foul,
Then would he whistle rapid as any lark,   495
Or carol some old roundelay, and so loud
That first they mock'd, but, after, reverenced him.
Or Gareth, telling some prodigious tale
Of knights who sliced a red life-bubbling way
Thro' twenty folds of twisted dragon, held   500
All in a gap-mouth'd circle his good mates
Lying or sitting round him, idle hands,
Charm'd; till Sir Kay, the seneschal, would come
Blustering upon them, like a sudden wind
Among dead leaves, and drive them all apart.   505
Or when the thralls had sport among themselves,
So there were any trial of mastery,
He, by two yards in casting bar or stone,
Was counted best; and if there chanced a joust,
So that Sir Kay nodded him leave to go,   510

Would hurry thither, and when he saw the knights
Clash like the coming and retiring wave,
And the spear spring, and good horse reel, the boy
Was half beyond himself for ecstasy.

So for a month he wrought among the thralls;   515
But in the weeks that follow'd, the good Queen,
Repentant of the word she made him swear,
And saddening in her childless castle, sent,
Between the in-crescent and de-crescent moon,
Arms for her son, and loosed him from his vow.   520

This, Gareth hearing from a squire of Lot
With whom he used to play at tourney once,
When both were children, and in lonely haunts
Would scratch a ragged oval on the sand,
And each at either dash from either end—   525
Shame never made girl redder than Gareth joy.
He laugh'd; he sprang. "Out of the smoke, at
          once
I leap from Satan's foot to Peter's knee—
These news be mine, none other's—nay, the King's—
Descend into the city:" whereon he sought   530
• The King alone, and found, and told him all.

"I have stagger'd thy strong Gawain in a tilt
For pastime; yea, he said it: joust can I.
Make me thy knight—in secret! let my name
Be hidden, and give me the first quest, I spring   535
Like flame from ashes."

Here the King's calm eye
Fell on, and check'd, and made him flush, and bow
Lowly, to kiss his hand, who answer'd him:
"Son, the good mother let me know thee here,
And sent her wish that I would yield thee thine.   540
Make thee my knight? my knights are sworn to
        vows
Of utter hardihood, utter gentleness,
And, loving, utter faithfulness in love,
And uttermost obedience to the King."

Then Gareth, lightly springing from his knees: 545
"My King, for hardihood I can promise thee.
For uttermost obedience make demand
Of whom ye gave me to, the Seneschal,
No mellow master of the meats and drinks!
And as for love, God wot, I love not yet,   55C
But love I shall, God willing."

And the King:
"Make thee my knight in secret? yea, but he,
Our noblest brother, and our truest man,
And one with me in all, he needs must know."

"Let Lancelot know, my King, let Lancelot know,
Thy noblest and thy truest!"

And the King: 55t
"But wherefore would ye men should wonder at you?
Nay, rather for the sake of me, their King,

And the deed's sake my knighthood do the deed,
Than to be noised of."

          Merrily Gareth ask'd: 560
"Have I not earn'd my cake in baking of it?
Let be my name until I make my name!
My deeds will speak: it is but for a day."
So with a kindly hand on Gareth's arm
Smiled the great King, and half-unwillingly   565
Loving his lusty youthhood yielded to him.
Then, after summoning Lancelot privily:
"I have given him the first quest: he is not proven.
Look therefore, when he calls for this in hall,
Thou get to horse and follow him far away.   570
Cover the lions on thy shield, and see,
Far as thou mayest, he be nor ta'en nor slain."

  Then that same day there past into the hall
A damsel of high lineage, and a brow
May-blossom, and a cheek of apple-blossom,   575
Hawk-eyes; and lightly was her slender nose
Tip-tilted like the petal of a flower:
She into hall past with her page and cried:

  "O King, for thou hast driven the foe without,
See to the foe within! bridge, ford, beset   580
By bandits, every one that owns a tower
The lord for half a league.   Why sit ye there?
Rest would I not, Sir King, an I were king,
Till even the lonest hold were all as free

From cursed bloodshed as thine altar-cloth   585
From that best blood it is a sin to spill."

"Comfort thyself," said Arthur, "I nor mine
Rest: so my knighthood keep the vows they swore,
The wastest moorland of our realm shall be
Safe, damsel, as the centre of this hall.   590
What is thy name? thy need?"

                        "My name?" she said—
"Lynette, my name; noble; my need, a knight
To combat for my sister, Lyonors,
A lady of high lineage, of great lands,
And comely, yea, and comelier than myself.   595
She lives in Castle Perilous: a river
Runs in three loops about her living-place;
And o'er it are three passings, and three knights
Defend the passings, brethren, and a fourth,
And of that four the mightiest, holds her stay'd   600
In her own castle, and so besieges her
To break her will, and make her wed with him;
And but delays his purport till thou send
To do the battle with him thy chief man
Sir Lancelot, whom he trusts to overthrow;   605
Then wed, with glory: but she will not wed
Save whom she loveth, or a holy life.
Now therefore have I came for Lancelot."

Then Arthur mindful of Sir Gareth ask'd:
"Damsel, ye know this Order lives to crush   610

All wrongers of the realm. But say, these four,
Who be they? What the fashion of the men?"

"They be of foolish fashion, O Sir King,
The fashion of that old knight-errantry
Who ride abroad, and do but what they will;   615
Courteous or bestial from the moment, such
As have nor law nor king; and three of these
Proud in their fantasy call themselves the Day,
Morning-Star, and Noon-Sun, and Evening-Star,
Being strong fools; and never a whit more wise   620
The fourth, who alway rideth arm'd in black,
A huge man-beast of boundless savagery.
He names himself the Night and oftener Death,
And wears a helmet mounted with a skull,
And bears a skeleton figured on his arms,   625
To show that who may slay or scape the three,
Slain by himself, shall enter endless night.
And all these four be fools, but mighty men,
And therefore am I come for Lancelot."

Hereat Sir Gareth call'd from where he rose,   630
A head with kindling eyes above the throng,
"A boon, Sir King—this quest!" then—for he mark'd
Kay near him groaning like a wounded bull—
"Yea, King, thou knowest thy kitchen-knave am I,
And mighty thro' thy meats and drinks am I,   635
And I can topple over a hundred such.
Thy promise, King," and Arthur glancing at him,
Brought down a momentary brow. "Rough, sudden,

And pardonable, worthy to be knight—
Go therefore," and all hearers were amazed.   640

But on the damsel's forehead shame, pride, wrath
Slew the may-white: she lifted either arm,
"Fie on thee, King! I ask'd for thy chief knight,
And thou hast given me but a kitchen-knave."
Then ere a man in hall could stay her, turn'd,   645
Fled down the lane of access to the King,
Took horse, descended the slope street, and past
The weird white gate, and paused without, beside
The field of tourney, murmuring "kitchen-knave!"

Now two great entries open'd from the hall,   650
At one end one that gave upon a range
Of level pavement where the King would pace
At sunrise, gazing over plain and wood;
And down from this a lordly stairway sloped
Till lost in blowing trees and tops of towers;   655
And out by this main doorway past the King.
But one was counter to the hearth, and rose
High that the highest-crested helm could ride
Therethro' nor graze; and by this entry fled
The damsel in her wrath, and on to this   660
Sir Gareth strode, and saw without the door
King Arthur's gift, the worth of half a town,
A war-horse of the best, and near it stood
The two that out of north had follow'd him.
This bare a maiden shield, a casque; that held   665
The horse, the spear; whereat Sir Gareth loosed

A cloak that dropt from collar-bone to heel,
A cloth of roughest web, and cast it down,
And from it, like a fuel-smother'd fire
That lookt half-dead, brake bright, and flash'd as those
Dull-coated things, that making slide apart   671
Their dusk wing-cases, all beneath there burns
A jewell'd harness, ere they pass and fly.
So Gareth ere he parted flash'd in arms.
Then as he donn'd the helm, and took the shield   675
And mounted horse and graspt a spear, of grain
Storm-strengthen'd on a windy site, and tipt
With trenchant steel, around him slowly prest
The people, while from out of kitchen came
The thralls in throng, and seeing who had work'd   680
Lustier than any, and whom they could but love,
Mounted in arms, threw up their caps and cried,
"God bless the King, and all his fellowship!"
And on thro' lanes of shouting Gareth rode
Down the slope street, and past without the gate.   685

So Gareth past with joy; but as the cur
Pluckt from the cur he fights with, ere his cause
Be cool'd by fighting, follows, being named,
His owner, but remembers all, and growls
Remembering, so Sir Kay beside the door   690
Mutter'd in scorn of Gareth whom he used
To harry and hustle.

　　　　　　　　"Bound upon a quest
With horse and arms—the King hath past his time—

My scullion knave! Thralls, to your work again,
For an your fire be low ye kindle mine! 695
Will there be dawn in West and eve in East?
Begone!—my knave!—belike and like enow
Some old head-blow not heeded in his youth
So shook his wits they wander in his prime—
Crazed! How the villain lifted up his voice, 700
Nor shamed to bawl himself a kitchen-knave!
Tut, he was tame and meek enow with me,
Till peacock'd up with Lancelot's noticing.
Well—I will after my loud knave, and learn
Whether he know me for his master yet. 705
Out of the smoke he came, and so my lance
Hold, by God's grace, he shall into the mire—
Thence, if the King awaken from his craze,
Into the smoke again."

     But Lancelot said:
"Kay, wherefore wilt thou go against the King, 710
For that did never he whereon ye rail,
But ever meekly served the King in thee?
Abide: take counsel; for this lad is great
And lusty, and knowing both of lance and sword."
"Tut, tell not me," said Kay, "ye are overfine 715
To mar stout knaves with foolish courtesies:"
Then mounted, on thro' silent faces rode
Down the slope city, and out beyond the gate.

 But by the field of tourney lingering yet
Mutter'd the damsel: "Wherefore did the King 720

Scorn me? for, were Sir Lancelot lackt, at least
He might have yielded to me one of those
Who tilt for lady's love and glory here,
Rather than—O sweet heaven! O fie upon him!—
His kitchen-knave."

      To whom Sir Gareth drew—
And there were none but few goodlier than he—   726
Shining in arms, "Damsel, the quest is mine.
Lead, and I follow." She therat, as one
That smells a foul-flesh'd agaric in the holt,
And deems it carrion of some woodland thing,   730
Or shrew, or weasel, nipt her slender nose
With petulant thumb and finger, shrilling, "Hence!
Avoid, thou smellest all of kitchen-grease.
And look who comes behind;" for there was Kay.
"Knowest thou not me? thy master? I am Kay.   735
We lack thee by the hearth."

      And Gareth to him,
"Master no more! too well I know thee, ay—
The most ungentle knight in Arthur's hall."
"Have at thee then," said Kay: they shock'd, and Kay
Fell shoulder-slipt, and Gareth cried again,   740
"Lead, and I follow," and fast away she fled.

 But after sod and shingle ceased to fly
Behind her, and the heart of her good horse
Was nigh to burst with violence of the beat,
Perforce she stay'd, and overtaken spoke: 745

"What doest thou, scullion, in my fellowship?
Deem'st thou that I accept thee aught the more
Or love thee better, that by some device
Full cowardly, or by mere unhappiness,
Thou hast overthrown and slain thy master—thou!—
Dish-washer and broach-turner, loon!—to me   751
Thou smellest all of kitchen as before."

"Damsel," Sir Gareth answer'd gently, "say
Whate'er ye will, but whatsoe'er ye say,
I leave not till I finish this fair quest,   755
Or die therefore."

     "Ay, wilt thou finish it?
Sweet lord, how like a noble knight he talks!
The listening rogue hath caught the manner of it.
But, knave, anon thou shalt be met with, knave,
And then by such a one that thou for all   760
The kitchen brewis that was ever supt
Shalt not once dare to look him in the face."

"I shall assay," said Gareth with a smile
That madden'd her, and away she flash'd again
Down the long avenues of a boundless wood,   765
And Gareth following was again beknaved:

"Sir Kitchen-knave, I have miss'd the only way
Where Arthur's men are set along the wood;
The wood is nigh as full of thieves as leaves:
If both be slain, I am rid of thee; but yet,   770

Sir Scullion, canst thou use that spit of thine?
Fight, an thou canst: I have miss'd the only way."

So till the dusk that follow'd evensong
Rode on the two, reviler and reviled;
Then after one long slope was mounted, saw,   775
Bowl-shaped, thro' tops of many thousand pines
A gloomy-gladed hollow slowly sink
To westward—in the deeps whereof a mere,
Round as the red eye of an eagle-owl,
Under the half-dead sunset glared; and shouts   780
Ascended, and there brake a servingman
Flying from out of the black wood, and crying,
"They have bound my lord to cast him in the
        mere."
Then Gareth, "Bound am I to right the wrong'd,
But straitlier bound am I to bide with thee."   785
And when the damsel spake contemptuously,
"Lead, and I follow," Gareth cried again,
"Follow, I lead!" so down among the pines
He plunged; and there, black-shadow'd nigh the mere,
And mid-thigh-deep in bulrushes and reed,   790
Saw six tall men haling a seventh along,
A stone about his neck to drown him in it.
Three with good blows he quieted, but three
Fled thro' the pines; and Gareth loosed the stone
From off his neck, then in the mere beside   795
Tumbled it; oilily bubbled up the mere.
Last, Gareth loosed his bonds and on free feet
Set him, a stalwart baron, Arthur's friend.

"Well that ye came, or else these caitiff rogues
Had wreak'd themselves on me; good cause is theirs   800
To hate me, for my wont hath ever been
To catch my thief, and then like vermin here
Drown him, and with a stone about his neck;
And under this wan water many of them
Lie rotting, but at night let go the stone,   805
And rise, and flickering in a grimly light
Dance on the mere. Good now, ye have saved a
        life
Worth somewhat as the cleanser of this wood.
And fain would I reward thee worshipfully.
What guerdon will ye?"

                    Gareth sharply spake: 810
"None! for the deed's sake have I done the deed,
In uttermost obedience to the King.
But wilt thou yield this damsel harborage?"

    Whereat the baron saying, "I well believe
You be of Arthur's Table," a light laugh   815
Broke from Lynette: "Ay, truly of a truth,
And in a sort, being Arthur's kitchen-knave!—
But deem not I accept thee aught the more,
Scullion, for running sharply with thy spit
Down on a rout of craven foresters.   820
A thresher with his flail had scatter'd them.
Nay—for thou smellest of the kitchen still.
But an this lord will yield us harborage,
Well."

So she spake. A league beyond the wood,
All in a full-fair manor and a rich,   825
His towers, where that day a feast had been
Held in high hall, and many a viand left,
And many a costly cate, received the three.
And there they placed a peacock in his pride
Before the damsel, and the baron set   830
Gareth beside her, but at once she rose.

"Meseems, that here is much discourtesy,
Setting this knave, Lord Baron, at my side.
Hear me—this morn I stood in Arthur's hall,
And pray'd the King would grant me Lancelot   835
To fight the brotherhood of Day and Night—
The last a monster unsubduable
Of any save of him for whom I call'd—
Suddenly bawls this frontless kitchen-knave,
'The quest is mine; thy kitchen-knave am I,   840
And mighty thro' thy meats and drinks am I.'
Then Arthur all at once gone mad replies,
'Go therefore,' and so gives the quest to him—
Him—here—a villain fitter to stick swine
Than ride abroad redressing women's wrong,   845
Or sit beside a noble gentlewoman."

Then half-ashamed and part-amazed, the lord
Now look'd at one and now at other, left
The damsel by the peacock in his pride,
And, seating Gareth at another board,   850
Sat down beside him, ate and then began:

"Friend, whether thou be kitchen-knave, or not,
Or whether it be the maiden's fantasy,
And whether she be mad, or else the King,
Or both or neither, or thyself be mad,   855
I ask not: but thou strikest a strong stroke,
For strong thou art and goodly therewithal,
And saver of my life; and therefore now,
For here be mighty men to joust with, weigh
Whether thou wilt not with thy damsel back   860
To crave again Sir Lancelot of the King.
Thy pardon; I but speak for thine avail,
The saver of my life."

          And Gareth said,
"Full pardon, but I follow up the quest,
Despite of Day and Night and Death and Hell."   865

So when, next morn, the lord whose life he saved
Had, some brief space, convey'd them on their way
And left them with God-speed, Sir Gareth spake,
"Lead, and I follow." Haughtily she replied:

"I fly no more: I allow thee for an hour.   870
Lion and stoat have isled together, knave,
In time of flood. Nay, furthermore, methinks
Some ruth is mine for thee. Back wilt thou, fool?
For hard by here is one will overthrow
And slay thee; then will I to court again,   875
And shame the King for only yielding me
My champion from the ashes of his hearth."

To whom Sir Gareth answer'd courteously:
"Say thou thy say, and I will do my deed.
Allow me for mine hour, and thou wilt find   880
My fortunes all as fair as hers who lay
Among the ashes and wedded the King's son."

Then to the shore of one of those long loops
Wherethro' the serpent river coil'd, they came.
Rough-thicketed were the banks and steep; the stream
Full, narrow; this a bridge of single arc   886
Took at a leap; and on the further side
Arose a silk pavilion, gay with gold
In streaks and rays, and all Lent-lily in hue,
Save that the dome was purple, and above,   890
Crimson, a slender banneret fluttering.
And therebefore the lawless warrior paced
Unarm'd, and calling, "Damsel, is this he,
The champion thou hast brought from Arthur's hall?
For whom we let thee pass." "Nay, nay," she said,
"Sir Morning-Star. The King in utter scorn   896
Of thee and thy much folly hath sent thee here
His kitchen-knave: and look thou to thyself:
See that he fall not on thee suddenly,
And slay thee unarm'd; he is not knight but knave." 900

Then at his call, "O daughters of the Dawn,
And servants of the Morning-Star, approach,
Arm me," from out the silken curtain-folds
Bare-footed and bare-headed three fair girls
In gilt and rosy raiment came: their feet   905

In dewy grasses glisten'd; and the hair
All over glanced with dewdrop or with gem
Like sparkles in the stone Avanturine.
These arm'd him in blue arms, and gave a shield
Blue also, and thereon the morning star.   910
And Gareth silent gazed upon the knight,
Who stood a moment, ere his horse was brought,
Glorying; and in the stream beneath him shone,
Immingled with Heaven's azure waveringly,
The gay pavilion and the naked feet,   915
His arms, the rosy raiment, and the star.

Then she that watch'd him: "Wherefore stare ye
      so?
Thou shakest in thy fear: there yet is time:
Flee down the valley before he get to horse.
Who will cry shame? Thou art not knight but knave."

Said Gareth: "Damsel, whether knave or knight, 921
Far liefer had I fight a score of times
Than hear thee so missay me and revile.
Fair words were best for him who fights for thee;
But truly foul are better, for they send   925
That strength of anger thro' mine arms, I know
That I shall overthrow him."

                              And he that bore
The star, when mounted, cried from o'er the bridge:
"A kitchen-knave, and sent in scorn of me!
Such fight not I, but answer scorn with scorn.   930

For this were shame to do him further wrong
Than set him on his feet, and take his horse
And arms, and so return him to the King.
Come, therefore, leave thy lady lightly, knave.
Avoid: for it beseemeth not a knave   935
To ride with such a lady."

                    "Dog, thou liest!
I spring from loftier lineage than thine own."
He spake; and all at fiery speed the two
Shock'd on the central bridge, and either spear
Bent but not brake, and either knight at once, 940
Hurl'd as a stone from out of a catapult
Beyond his horse's crupper and the bridge,
Fell, as if dead; but quickly rose and drew,
And Gareth lash'd so fiercely with his brand
He drave his enemy backward down the bridge,   945
The damsel crying, "Well-stricken, kitchen-knave!"
Till Gareth's shield was cloven; but one stroke
Laid him that clove it grovelling on the ground.

   Then cried the fallen, "Take not my life: I yield."
And Gareth, "So this damsel ask it of me   950
Good—I accord it easily as a grace."
She reddening, "Insolent scullion! I of thee?
I bound to thee for any favor ask'd!"
"Then shall he die."   And Gareth there unlaced
His helmet as to slay him, but she shriek'd,   955
"Be not so hardy, scullion, as to slay
One nobler than thyself."   "Damsel, thy charge

Is an abounding pleasure to me. Knight,
Thy life is thine at her command. Arise
And quickly pass to Arthur's hall, and say   960
His kitchen-knave hath sent thee. See thou crave
His pardon for thy breaking of his laws.
Myself when I return will plead for thee.
Thy shield is mine—farewell; and, damsel, thou,
Lead, and I follow."

          And fast away she fled;   965
Then when he came upon her, spake: "Methought,
Knave, when I watch'd thee striking on the bridge,
The savor of thy kitchen came upon me
A little faintlier: but the wind hath changed;
I scent it twenty-fold." And then she sang,   970
"'O morning star'—not that tall felon there
Whom thou, by sorcery or unhappiness
Or some device, hast foully overthrown,—
'O morning star that smilest in the blue,
O star, my morning dream hath proven true,   975
Smile sweetly, thou! my love hath smiled on me.'

"But thou begone, take counsel, and away,
For hard by here is one that guards a ford—
The second brother in their fool's parable—
Will pay thee all thy wages, and to boot.   980
Care not for shame: thou art not knight but knave."

To whom Sir Gareth answer'd, laughingly:
"Parables? Hear a parable of the knave.

When I was kitchen-knave among the rest,
Fierce was the hearth, and one of my co-mates   985
Own'd a rough dog, to whom he cast his coat,
'Guard it,' and there was none to meddle with it.
And such a coat art thou, and thee the King
Gave me to guard, and such a dog am I,
To worry, and not to flee—and—knight or knave—   990
The knave that doth thee service as full knight
Is all as good, meseems, as any knight
Toward thy sister's freeing."

                       "Ay, Sir Knave!
Ay, knave, because thou strikest as a knight,
Being but knave, I hate thee all the more."   995

   "Fair damsel, you should worship me the more,
That, being but knave, I throw thine enemies."

   "Ay, ay," she said, "but thou shalt meet thy match."

   So when they touch'd the second river-loop,
Huge on a huge red horse, and all in mail   1000
Burnish'd to blinding, shone the Noonday Sun
Beyond a raging shallow.   As if the flower
That blows a globe of after arrowlets
Ten-thousand-fold had grown, flash'd the fierce shield,
All sun; and Gareth's eyes had flying blots   1005
Before them when he turn'd from watching him.
He from beyond the roaring shallow roar'd,
"What doest thou, brother, in my marches here?"

And she athwart the shallow shrill'd again,
"Here is a kitchen-knave from Arthur's hall   1010
Hath overthrown thy brother, and hath his arms."
"Ugh!" cried the Sun, and vizoring up a red
And cipher face of rounded foolishness,
Push'd horse across the foamings of the ford,
Whom Gareth met mid-stream: no room was there   1015
For lance or tourney-skill: four strokes they struck
With sword, and these were mighty; the new knight
Had fear he might be shamed; but as the Sun
Heaved up a ponderous arm to strike the fifth,
The hoof of his horse slipt in the stream, the stream   1020
Descended, and the Sun was wash'd away.

   Then Gareth laid his lance athwart the ford;
So drew him home; but he that fought no more,
As being all bone-batter'd on the rock,
Yielded; and Gareth sent him to the King.   1025
"Myself when I return will plead for thee.
Lead, and I follow."   Quietly she led.
"Hath not the good wind, damsel, changed again?"
"Nay, not a point; nor art thou victor here.
There lies a ridge of slate across the ford;   1030
His horse thereon stumbled—ay, for I saw it.

   "'O sun'—not this strong fool whom thou, Sir Knave,
Hast overthrown thro' mere unhappiness—
'O sun, that wakenest all to bliss or pain,
O moon, that layest all to sleep again,   1035
Shine sweetly: twice my love hath smiled on me.'

"What knowest thou of love-song or of love?
Nay, nay, God wot, so thou wert nobly born,
Thou hast a pleasant presence. Yea, perchance,—

"'O dewy flowers that open to the sun,   1040
O dewy flowers that close when day is done,
Blow sweetly: twice my love hath smiled on me.'

"What knowest thou of flowers, except, belike,
To garnish meats with? hath not our good King
Who lent me thee, the flower of kitchendom,   1045
A foolish love for flowers? what stick ye round
The pasty? wherewithal deck the boar's head?
Flowers? nay, the boar hath rosemaries and bay.

"'O birds that warble to the morning sky,
O birds that warble as the day goes by,   1050
Sing sweetly: twice my love hath smiled on me.'

"What knowest thou of birds, lark, mavis, merle,
Linnet? what dream ye when they utter forth
May-music growing with the growing light,
Their sweet sun-worship? these be for the snare—   1055
So runs thy fancy—these be for the spit,
Larding and basting. See thou have not now
Larded thy last, except thou turn and fly.
There stands the third fool of their allegory."

For there beyond a bridge of treble bow,   1060
All in a rose-red from the west, and all

Naked it seem'd, and glowing in the broad
Deep-dimpled current underneath, the knight
That named himself the Star of Evening stood.

And Gareth, "Wherefore waits the madman there
Naked in open dayshine?" "Nay," she cried,   1066
"Not naked, only wrapt in harden'd skins
That fit him like his own; and so ye cleave
His armor off him, these will turn the blade."

Then the third brother shouted o'er the bridge,   1070
"O brother-star, why shine ye here so low?
Thy ward is higher up: but have ye slain
The damsel's champion?" and the damsel cried:

"No star of thine, but shot from Arthur's heaven
With all disaster unto thine and thee!   1075
For both thy younger brethren have gone down
Before this youth; and so wilt thou, Sir Star;
Art thou not old?"

            "Old, damsel, old and hard,
Old, with the might and breath of twenty boys."
Said Gareth, "Old, and over-bold in brag!   1080
But that same strength which threw the Morning Star
Can throw the Evening."

               Then that other blew
A hard and deadly note upon the horn.
"Approach and arm me!" With slow steps from out

An old storm-beaten, russet, many-stain'd   1085
Pavilion, forth a grizzled damsel came,
And arm'd him in old arms, and brought a helm
With but a drying evergreen for crest,
And gave a shield whereon the star of even
Half-tarnish'd and half-bright, his emblem, shone.   1090
But when it glitter'd o'er the saddle-bow,
They madly hurl'd together on the bridge;
And Gareth overthrew him, lighted, drew,
There met him drawn, and overthrew him again,
But up like fire he started: and as oft   1095
As Gareth brought him grovelling on his knees,
So many a time he vaulted up again;
Till Gareth panted hard, and his great heart,
Foredooming all his trouble was in vain,
Labor'd within him, for he seem'd as one   1100
That all in later, sadder age begins
To war against ill uses of a life,
But these from all his life arise, and cry,
"Thou hast made us lords, and canst not put us down!"
He half despairs; so Gareth seem'd to strike   1105
Vainly, the damsel clamoring all the while,
"Well done, knave-knight, well stricken, O good knight-
     knave—
O knave, as noble as any of all the knights—
Shame me not, shame me not. I have prophesied—
Strike, thou art worthy of the Table Round—   1110
His arms are old, he trusts the harden'd skin—
Strike—strike—the wind will never change again."
And Gareth hearing ever stronglier smote,

And hew'd great pieces of his armor off him,
But lash'd in vain against the harden'd skin,   1115
And could not wholly bring him under, more
Than loud Southwesterns, rolling ridge on ridge,
The buoy that rides at sea, and dips and springs
For ever; till at length Sir Gareth's brand
Clash'd his, and brake it utterly to the hilt.   1120
"I have thee now"; but forth that other sprang,
And, all unknightlike, writhed his wiry arms
Around him, till he felt, despite his mail,
Strangled, but straining even his uttermost
Cast, and so hurl'd him headlong o'er the bridge   1125
Down to the river, sink or swim, and cried,
"Lead, and I follow."

           But the damsel said:
"I lead no longer; ride thou at my side;
Thou art the kingliest of all kitchen-knaves.

  "'O trefoil, sparkling on the rainy plain,   1130
O rainbow with three colors after rain,
Shine sweetly: thrice my love hath smiled on me.'

  "Sir,—and, good faith, I fain had added—Knight,
But that I heard thee call thyself a knave,—
Shamed am I that I so rebuked, reviled,   1135
Missaid thee; noble I am; and thought the King
Scorn'd me and mine; and now thy pardon, friend,
For thou hast ever answer'd courteously,
And wholly bold thou art, and meek withal

As any of Arthur's best, but, being knave,　　1140
Hast mazed my wit: I marvel what thou art."

"Damsel," he said, "you be not all to blame,
Saving that you mistrusted our good King
Would handle scorn, or yield you, asking, one
Not fit to cope your quest. You said your say;　　1145
Mine answer was my deed. Good sooth! I hold
He scarce is knight, yea but half-man, nor meet
To fight for gentle damsel, he, who lets
His heart be stirr'd with any foolish heat
At any gentle damsel's waywardness.　　1150
Shamed? care not! thy foul sayings fought for me·
And seeing now thy words are fair, methinks
There rides no knight, not Lancelot, his great self,
Hath force to quell me."

　　　　　　　　　　　Nigh upon that hour
When the lone hern forgets his melancholy,　　1155
Lets down his other leg, and stretching dreams
Of goodly supper in the distant pool,
Then turn'd the noble damsel smiling at him,
And told him of a cavern hard at hand,
Where bread and baken meats and good red wine　1160
Of Southland, which the Lady Lyonors
Had sent her coming champion, waited him.

Anon they past a narrow comb wherein
Were slabs of rock with figures, knights on horse
Sculptured, and deckt in slowly-waning hues.　　1165

"Sir Knave, my knight, a hermit once was here,
Whose holy hand hath fashion'd on the rock
The war of Time against the soul of man.
And yon four fools have suck'd their allegory
From these damp walls, and taken but the form.   1176
Know ye not these?" and Gareth lookt and read—
In letters like to those the vexillary
Hath left crag-carven o'er the streaming Gelt—
"PHOSPHORUS," then "MERIDIES,"—"HESPERUS"—
"NOX"—"MORS," beneath five figures, armed men,
Slab after slab, their faces forward all,   1176
And running down the Soul, a shape that fled
With broken wings, torn raiment, and loose hair,
For help and shelter to the hermit's cave.
"Follow the faces, and we find it. Look,   1180
Who comes behind?"

                    For one—delay'd at first
Thro' helping back the dislocated Kay
To Camelot, then by what thereafter chanced,
The damsel's headlong error thro' the wood—
Sir Lancelot, having swum the river-loops—   1185
His blue shield-lions cover'd—softly drew
Behind the twain, and when he saw the star
Gleam, on Sir Gareth's turning to him, cried,
"Stay, felon knight, I avenge me for my friend."
And Gareth crying prick'd against the cry;   1190
But when they closed—in a moment—at one touch
Of that skill'd spear, the wonder of the world—
Went sliding down so easily, and fell.

That when he found the grass within his hands
He laugh'd; the laughter jarr'd upon Lynette: 1195
Harshly she ask'd him, "Shamed and overthrown,
And tumbled back into the kitchen-knave,
Why laugh ye? that ye blew your boast in vain?"
"Nay, noble damsel, but that I, the son
Of old King Lot and good Queen Bellicent,   1200
And victor of the bridges and the ford,
And knight of Arthur, here lie thrown by whom
I know not, all thro' mere unhappiness—
Device and sorcery and unhappiness—
Out, sword; we are thrown!" And Lancelot answer'd:
      "Prince,   1205
O Gareth—thro' the mere unhappiness
Of one who came to help thee, not to harm,
Lancelot, and all as glad to find thee whole
As on the day when Arthur knighted him."

Then Gareth: "Thou—Lancelot!—thine the hand 1210
That threw me? An some chance to mar the boast
Thy brethren of thee make—which could not chance—
Had sent thee down before a lesser spear,
Shamed had I been, and sad—O Lancelot—thou!"

Whereat the maiden, petulant: "Lancelot,   1215
Why came ye not, when call'd? and wherefore now
Come ye, not call'd? I gloried in my knave,
Who being still rebuked would answer still
Courteous as any knight—but now, if knight,
The marvel dies, and leaves me fool'd and trick'd,   1220

And only wondering wherefore play'd upon;
And doubtful whether I and mine be scorn'd.
Where should be truth if not in Arthur's hall,
In Arthur's presence? Knight, knave, prince and fool,
I hate thee and forever.''

          And Lancelot said: 1225
"Blessed be thou, Sir Gareth! knight art thou
To the King's best wish. O damsel, be you wise,
To call him shamed who is but overthrown?
Thrown have I been, nor once, but many a time.
Victor from vanquish'd issues at the last,   1230
And overthrower from being overthrown.
With sword we have not striven; and thy good horse
And thou are weary; yet not less I felt
Thy manhood thro' that wearied lance of thine.
Well hast thou done; for all the stream is freed,   1235
And thou hast wreak'd his justice on his foes,
And when reviled hast answer'd graciously,
And makest merry when overthrown. Prince, knight,
Hail, knight and prince, and of our Table Round!''

And then when turning to Lynette he told   1240
The tale of Gareth, petulantly she said:
"Ay, well—ay, well—for worse than being fool'd
Of others, is to fool one's self. A cave,
Sir Lancelot, is hard by, with meats and drinks
And forage for the horse, and flint for fire.   1245
But all about it flies a honeysuckle.
Seek, till we find.'' And when they sought and found,

Sir Gareth drank and ate, and all his life
Past into sleep; on whom the maiden gazed:
"Sound sleep be thine! sound cause to sleep hast thou.
Wake lusty! Seem I not as tender to him   125?
As any mother? Ay, but such a one
As all day long hath rated at her child,
And vext his day, but blesses him asleep—
Good lord, how sweetly smells the honeysuckle   1258
In the hush'd night, as if the world were one
Of utter peace, and love, and gentleness!
O Lancelot, Lancelot,"—and she clapt her hands—
"Full merry am I to find my goodly knave
Is knight and noble. See now, sworn have I,   1260
Else yon black felon had not let me pass,
To bring thee back to do the battle with him.
Thus an thou goest, he will fight thee first;
Who doubts thee victor? so will my knight-knave
Miss the full flower of this accomplishment."   1265

    Said Lancelot: "Peradventure he you name
May know my shield. Let Gareth, an he will,
Change his for mine, and take my charger, fresh,
Not to be spurr'd, loving the battle as well
As he that rides him." "Lancelot-like," she said,   1270
"Courteous in this, Lord Lancelot, as in all."

    And Gareth, wakening, fiercely clutch'd the shield:
"Ramp, ye lance-splintering lions, on whom all spears
Are rotten sticks! ye seem agape to roar!
Yea, ramp and roar at leaving of your lord!—   1275

Care not, good beasts, so well I care for you.
O noble Lancelot, from my hold on these
Streams virtue—fire—thro' one that will not shame
Even the shadow of Lancelot under shield.
Hence: let us go."

            Silent the silent field   1280
They traversed. Arthur's Harp tho' summer-wan,
In counter motion to the clouds, allured
The glance of Gareth dreaming on his liege.
A star shot: "Lo," said Gareth, "the foe falls!"
An owl whoopt: "Hark the victor pealing there!" 1285
Suddenly she that rode upon his left
Clung to the shield that Lancelot lent him, crying:
"Yield, yield him this again; 'tis he must fight:
I curse the tongue that all thro' yesterday
Reviled thee, and hath wrought on Lancelot now 1290
To lend thee horse and shield: wonders ye have done;
Miracles ye cannot: here is glory enow
In having flung the three: I see thee maim'd,
Mangled: I swear thou canst not fling the fourth."

  "And wherefore, damsel? tell me all ye know. 1295
You cannot scare me; nor rough face, or voice,
Brute bulk of limb, or boundless savagery
Appal me from the quest."

               "Nay, prince," she cried,
"God wot, I never look'd upon the face,
Seeing he never rides abroad by day;   1300

But watch'd him have I like a phantom pass
Chilling the night: nor have I heard the voice.
Always he made his mouthpiece of a page
Who came and went, and still reported him
As closing in himself the strength of ten, 1305
And when his anger tare him, massacring
Man, woman, lad, and girl—yea, the soft babe!
Some hold that he hath swallow'd infant flesh,
Monster! O prince, I went for Lancelot first,
The quest is Lancelot's: give him back the shield." 1310

Said Gareth laughing, "An he fight for this,
Belike he wins it as the better man:
Thus—and not else!"

But Lancelot on him urged
All the devisings of their chivalry
When one might meet a mightier than himself; 1315
How best to manage horse, lance, sword, and shield,
And so fill up the gap where force might fail
With skill and fineness. Instant were his words.

Then Gareth: "Here be rules. I know but one—
To dash against mine enemy and to win. 1320
Yet have I watch'd thee victor in the joust,
And seen thy way." "Heaven help thee!" sigh'd
Lynette.

Then for a space, and under cloud that grew
To thunder-gloom palling all stars, they rode

In converse till she made her palfrey halt,   1325
Lifted an arm, and softly whisper'd, "There."
And all the three were silent seeing, pitch'd
Beside the Castle Perilous on flat field,
A huge pavilion like a mountain peak
Sunder the glooming crimson on the marge,   1330
Black, with black banner, and a long black horn
Beside it hanging; which Sir Gareth graspt,
And so, before the two could hinder him,
Sent all his heart and breath thro' all the horn.
Echo'd the walls; a light twinkled; anon   1335
Came lights and lights, and once again he blew;
Whereon were hollow tramplings up and down
And muffled voices heard, and shadows past;
Till high above him, circled with her maids,
The Lady Lyonors at a window stood,   1340
Beautiful among lights, and waving to him
White hands and courtesy; but when the prince
Three times had blown—after long hush—at last—
The huge pavilion slowly yielded up,
Thro' those black foldings, that which housed therein.
High on a night-black horse, in night-black arms, 1346
With white breast-bone, and barren ribs of Death,
And crown'd with fleshless laughter—some ten steps—
In the half-light—thro' the dim dawn—advanced
The monster, and then paused, and spake no word. 1350

But Gareth spake and all indignantly:
"Fool, for thou hast, men say, the strength of ten,
Canst thou not trust the limbs thy God hath given,

But must, to make the terror of thee more,
Trick thyself out in ghastly imageries   1355
Of that which Life hath done with, and the clod,
Less dull than thou, will hide with mantling flowers
As if for pity?" But he spake no word;
Which set the horror higher: a maiden swoon'd;
The Lady Lyonors wrung her hands and wept,   1360
As doom'd to be the bride of Night and Death;
Sir Gareth's head prickled beneath his helm;
And even Sir Lancelot thro' his warm blood felt
Ice strike, and all that mark'd him were aghast.

At once Sir Lancelot's charger fiercely neigh'd,   1365
And Death's dark war-horse bounded forward with him.
Then those that did not blink the terror saw
That Death was cast to ground, and slowly rose.
But with one stroke Sir Gareth split the skull.
Half fell to right and half to left and lay.   1370
Then with a stronger buffet he clove the helm
As throughly as the skull; and out from this
Issued the bright face of a blooming boy
Fresh as a flower new-born, and crying, "Knight,
Slay me not: my three brethren bade me do it,   1375
To make a horror all about the house,
And stay the world from Lady Lyonors;
They never dream'd the passes would be past."
Answer'd Sir Gareth graciously to one
Not many a moon his younger, "My fair child,   1380
What madness made thee challenge the chief knight
Of Arthur's hall?" "Fair Sir, they bade me do it.

They hate the King and Lancelot, the King's friend;
They hoped to slay him somewhere on the stream,
They never dream'd the passes could be past."   1385

   Then sprang the happier day from underground;
And Lady Lyonors and her house, with dance
And revel and song, made merry over Death,
As being after all their foolish fears
And horrors only proven a blooming boy.   1390
So large mirth lived, and Gareth won the quest.

   And he that told the tale in older times
Says that Sir Gareth wedded Lyonors,
But he that told it later says Lynette.

LANCELOT AND ELAINE

From Gareth and Lynette to Lancelot and Elaine

It is a far cry from the wholesome atmosphere of "Gareth and Lynette" to the sin-ladened mist of "Lancelot and Elaine." In reading the complete cycle, there is not the abrupt transition that is found in following the order of the present edition.

"The Marriage of Geraint," and "Geraint and Enid" were originally published as a single poem following "Gareth and Lynette." Here,—

> "a rumor rose about the Queen,
> Touching her guilty love for Lancelot,
> Tho' yet there lived no proof."

This rumor is believed by Geraint, who fears that his wife has been contaminated by her association with the Queen. Though the suspicion causes great suffering, it does no permanent harm.

In the next Idyll, "Balin and Balan," the results of the sin are more tragic. Balin takes the Queen and Lancelot as embodiments of his ideals, and when he becomes convinced of their perfidy, he draws the natural though unwarranted conclusion that there is neither honor in man nor purity in woman. In the madness of his despair, he engages in a deadly combat with his gentler brother, Balan, whom he meets unknown in the woods. Each brother mortally wounds the other; then each recognizes his opponent and they die in each other's arms.

"Balin and Balan" serves to introduce the bright baleful star, Vivien, a woman thoroughly bad without the extenuating love of

96

Guinevere. She comes to the court, which in Gareth's time would have repelled her, makes wicked lightnings of her eyes, and strikes down Merlin, Arthur's mage, the type of earthly wisdom.

In "Lancelot and Elaine" the sin spreads out as a blackening cloud and brings death to the innocent Elaine. Elaine, living in fantasy, is the Lady of Shalott over again. She is happy until she sees Sir Lancelot. "The pure heart of youth has lovelier imaginations than any experience of life can bring, sweeter and more varied fantasies than any genius that has sinned and sorrowed. But they are always silent."—Stopford Brooke.

ELAINE the fair, Elaine the lovable,
Elaine, the lily maid of Astolat,
High in her chamber up a tower to the east
Guarded the sacred shield of Lancelot;
Which first she placed where morning's earliest ray   5
Might strike it, and awake her with the gleam;
Then fearing rust or soilure fashion'd for it
A case of silk, and braided thereupon
All the devices blazon'd on the shield
In their own tinct, and added, of her wit,   10
A border fantasy of branch and flower,
And yellow-throated nestling in the nest.
Nor rested thus content, but day by day,
Leaving her household and good father, climb'd
That eastern tower, and entering barr'd her door,   15
Stript off the case, and read the naked shield,
Now guess'd a hidden meaning in his arms,
Now made a pretty history to herself
Of every dint a sword had beaten in it,
And every scratch a lance had made upon it,   20
Conjecturing when and where: this cut is fresh;

That ten years back; this dealt him at Caerlyle;
That at Caerleon; this at Camelot:
And ah, God's mercy, what a stroke was there!
And here a thrust that might have kill'd, but God   25
Broke the strong lance, and roll'd his enemy down,
And saved him: so she lived in fantasy.

End Of Setting

How came the lily maid by that good shield
Of Lancelot, she that knew not even his name?
He left it with her, when he rode to tilt   30
For the great diamond in the diamond jousts,
Which Arthur had ordain'd, and by that name
Had named them, since a diamond was the prize.

For Arthur, long before they crown'd him King,
Roving the trackless realms of Lyonnesse,   35
Had found a glen, gray boulder and black tarn.
A horror lived about the tarn, and clave
Like its own mists to all the mountain side:
For here two brothers, one a king, had met
And fought together; but their names were lost;   40
And each had slain his brother at a blow;
And down they fell and made the glen abhorr'd:
And there they lay till all their bones were bleach'd,
And lichen'd into color with the crags:
And he that once was king had on a crown   45
Of diamonds, one in front and four aside.
And Arthur came, and laboring up the pass,
All in a misty moonshine, unawares
Had trodden that crown'd skeleton, and the skull

Brake from the nape, and from the skull the crown　50
Roll'd into light, and turning on its rims
Fled like a glittering rivulet to the tarn:
And down the shingly scaur he plunged, and caught,
And set it on his head, and in his heart
Heard murmurs, "Lo, thou likewise shalt be king."　55

　　Thereafter, when a king, he had the gems
Pluck'd from the crown, and show'd them to his knights
Saying: "These jewels, whereupon I chanced
Divinely, are the kingdom's, not the King's—
For public use: henceforward let there be,　　60
Once every year, a joust for one of these:
For so by nine years' proof we needs must learn
Which is our mightiest, and ourselves shall grow
In use of arms and manhood, till we drive
The heathen, who, some say, shall rule the land　65
Hereafter, which God hinder!" Thus he spoke:
And eight years past, eight jousts had been, and still
Had Lancelot won the diamond of the year,
With purpose to present them to the Queen
When all were won; but, meaning all at once　70
To snare her royal fancy with a boon
Worth half her realm, had never spoken word.

　　Now for the central diamond and the last
And largest, Arthur, holding then his court
Hard on the river nigh the place which now　75
Is this world's hugest, let proclaim a joust
At Camelot, and when the time drew nigh

Spake—for she had been sick—to Guinevere:
"Are you so sick, my Queen, you cannot move
To these fair jousts?" "Yea, lord," she said, "ye know
   it."   80
"Then will ye miss," he answer'd, "the great deeds
Of Lancelot, and his prowess in the lists,
A sight ye love to look on." And the Queen
Lifted her eyes, and they dwelt languidly
On Lancelot, where he stood beside the King.   85
He, thinking that he read her meaning there,
"Stay with me, I am sick; my love is more
Than many diamonds," yielded; and a heart
Love-loyal to the least wish of the Queen—
However much he yearn'd to make complete   90
The tale of diamonds for his destined boon—
Urged him to speak against the truth, and say,
"Sir King, mine ancient wound is hardly whole,
And lets me from the saddle;" and the King
Glanced first at him, then her, and went his way. 95
No sooner gone than suddenly she began:

   "To blame, my lord Sir Lancelot, much to blame!
Why go ye not to these fair jousts? the knights
Are half of them our enemies, and the crowd
Will murmur, 'Lo the shameless ones, who take   100
Their pastime now the trustful King is gone!'"
Then Lancelot, vext at having lied in vain:
"Are ye so wise? ye were not once so wise,
My Queen, that summer when ye loved me first.
Then of the crowd ye took no more account   105

Than of the myriad cricket of the mead,
When its own voice clings to each blade of grass,
And every voice is nothing. As to knights,
Them surely can I silence with all ease.
But now my loyal worship is allow'd   110
Of all men: many a bard, without offence,
Has link'd our names together in his lay,
Lancelot, the flower of bravery, Guinevere,
The pearl of beauty; and our knights at feast
Have pledged us in this union, while the King   115
Would listen smiling. How then? is there more?
Has Arthur spoken aught? or would yourself,
Now weary of my service and devoir,
Henceforth be truer to your faultless lord?"

    She broke into a little scornful laugh: 120
"Arthur, my lord, Arthur, the faultless King,
That passionate perfection, my good lord—
But who can gaze upon the sun in heaven?
He never spake word of reproach to me,
He never had a glimpse of mine untruth,   125
He cares not for me: only here to-day
There gleamed a vague suspicion in his eyes:
Some meddling rogue has tamper'd with him—else
Rapt in this fancy of his Table Round,
And swearing men to vows impossible,   130
To make them like himself; but, friend, to me
He is all fault who hath no fault at all:
For who loves me must have a touch of earth;
The low sun makes the color: I am yours,

Not Arthur's, as ye know, save by the bond.　135
And therefore hear my words: go to the jousts:
The tiny-trumpeting gnat can break our dream
When sweetest; and the vermin voices here
May buzz so loud—we scorn them, but they sting."

Then answer'd Lancelot, the chief of knights:　140
"And with what face, after my pretext made,
Shall I appear, O Queen, at Camelot, I
Before a king who honors his own word
As if it were his God's?"

　　　　　　　　"Yea," said the Queen,
"A moral child without the craft to rule,　145
Else had he not lost me: but listen to me,
If I must find you wit: we hear it said
That men go down before your spear at a touch,
But knowing you are Lancelot; your great name,
This conquers: hide it therefore; go unknown:　150
Win! by this kiss you will: and our true King
Will then allow your pretext, O my knight,
As all for glory; for to speak him true,
Ye know right well, how meek soe'er he seem,
No keener hunter after glory breathes.　155
He loves it in his knights more than himself;
They prove to him his work: win and return."

Then got Sir Lancelot suddenly to horse,
Wroth at himself. Not willing to be known,
He left the barren-beaten thoroughfare,　160

Chose the green path that show'd the rarer foot,
And there among the solitary downs,
Full often lost in fancy, lost his way;
Till as he traced a faintly-shadow'd track,
That all in loops and links among the dales   165
Ran to the Castle of Astolat, he saw
Fired from the west, far on a hill, the towers.
Thither he made, and blew the gateway horn.
Then came an old, dumb, myriad-wrinkled man,
Who let him into lodging and disarm'd.   170
And Lancelot marvell'd at the wordless man;
And issuing found the Lord of Astolat
With two strong sons, Sir Torre and Sir Lavàine,
Moving to meet him in the castle court;
And close behind them stept the lily maid   175
Elaine, his daughter: mother of the house
There was not. Some light jest among them rose
With laughter dying down as the great knight
Approach'd them; then the Lord of Astolat:
"Whence comest thou, my guest, and by what
        name   180
Livest between the lips? for by thy state
And presence I might guess thee chief of those,
After the King, who eat in Arthur's halls.
Him have I seen: the rest, his Table Round,
Known as they are, to me they are unknown."   185

    Then answer'd Lancelot, the chief of knights:
"Known am I, and of Arthur's hall, and known,
What I by mere mischance have brought, my shield.

But since I go to joust as one unknown
At Camelot for the diamond, ask me not;   190
Hereafter ye shall know me—and the shield—
I pray you lend me one, if such you have,
Blank, or at least with some device not mine."

Then said the Lord of Astolat: "Here is Torre's:
Hurt in his first tilt was my son, Sir Torre;   195
And so, God wot, his shield is blank enough.
His ye can have."   Then added plain Sir Torre,
"Yea, since I cannot use it, ye may have it."
Here laugh'd the father saying: "Fie, Sir Churl,
Is that an answer for a noble knight?   200
Allow him! but Lavaine, my younger here,
He is so full of lustihood, he will ride,
Joust for it, and win, and bring it in an hour,
And set it in this damsel's golden hair,
To make her thrice as wilful as before."   205

"Nay, father, nay, good father, shame me not
Before this noble knight," said young Lavaine,
"For nothing.   Surely I but play'd on Torre:
He seem'd so sullen, vext he could not go:
A jest, no more! for, knight, the maiden dreamt   210
That some one put this diamond in her hand,
And that it was too slippery to be held,
And slipt and fell into some pool or stream,
The castle-well, belike; and then I said
That *if* I went and *if* I fought and won it—   215
But all was jest and joke among ourselves—

Then must she keep it safelier. All was jest.
But, father, give me leave, an if he will,
To ride to Camelot with this noble knight:
Win shall I not, but do my best to win; 220
Young as I am, yet would I do my best."

"So ye will grace me," answer'd Lancelot,
Smiling a moment, "with your fellowship
O'er these waste downs whereon I lost myself,
Then were I glad of you as guide and friend: 225
And you shall win this diamond,—as I hear,
It is a fair large diamond,—if ye may,
And yield it to this maiden, if ye will."
"A fair large diamond," added plain Sir Torre,
"Such be for queens, and not for simple maids." 230
Then she, who held her eyes upon the ground,
Elaine, and heard her name so tost about,
Flush'd slightly at the slight disparagement
Before the stranger knight, who, looking at her,
Full courtly, yet not falsely, thus return'd: 235
"If what is fair be but for what is fair,
And only queens are to be counted so,
Rash were my judgment then, who deem this maid
Might wear as fair a jewel as is on earth,
Not violating the bond of like to like." 240

He spoke and ceased: the lily maid Elaine,
Won by the mellow voice before she look'd,
Lifted her eyes and read his lineaments.
The great and guilty love he bare the Queen,

In battle with the love he bare his lord,   245
Had marr'd his face, and mark'd it ere his time.
Another sinning on such heights with one,
The flower of all the west and all the world,
Had been the sleeker for it; but in him
His mood was often like a fiend, and rose   250
And drove him into wastes and solitudes
For agony, who was yet a living soul.
Marr'd as he was, he seem'd the goodliest man
That ever among ladies ate in hall,
And noblest, when she lifted up her eyes.   255
However marr'd, of more than twice her years,
Seam'd with an ancient sword-cut on the cheek,
And bruised and bronzed, she lifted up her eyes
And loved him, with that love which was her doom.

   Then the great knight, the darling of the court,   260
Loved of the loveliest, into that rude hall
Stept with all grace, and not with half disdain
Hid under grace, as in a smaller time,
But kindly man moving among his kind:
Whom they with meats and vintage of their best   265
And talk and minstrel melody entertain'd.
And much they ask'd of court and Table Round,
And ever well and readily answer'd he;
But Lancelot, when they glanced at Guinevere,
Suddenly speaking of the wordless man,   270
Heard from the baron that, ten years before,
The heathen caught and reft him of his tongue.
"He learnt and warn'd me of their fierce design

Against my house, and him they caught and maim'd;
But I, my sons, and little daughter fled   275
From bonds or death, and dwelt among the woods
By the great river in a boatman's hut.
Dull days were those, till our good Arthur broke
The Pagan yet once more on Badon hill."

"O there, great lord, doubtless," Lavaine said, rapt
By all the sweet and sudden passion of youth   281
Toward greatness in its elder, "you have fought.
O, tell us—for we live apart—you know
Of Arthur's glorious wars." And Lancelot spoke
And answer'd him at full, as having been   285
With Arthur in the fight which all day long
Rang by the white mouth of the violent Glem;
And in the four loud battles by the shore
Of Duglas; that on Bassa; then the war
That thunder'd in and out the gloomy skirts   290
Of Celidon the forest; and again
By Castle Gurnion, where the glorious King
Had on his cuirass worn our Lady's Head,
Carved of one emerald centred in a sun
Of silver rays, that lighten'd as he breathed;   295
And at Caerleon had he helped his lord,
When the strong neighings of the wild White Horse
Set every gilded parapet shuddering;
And up in Agned-Cathregonion too,
And down the waste sand-shores of Trath Treroit,   300
Where many a heathen fell; "and on the mount
Of Badon I myself beheld the King

Charge at the head of all his Table Round,
And all his legions crying Christ and him,
And break them; and I saw him, after, stand   305
High on a heap of slain, from spur to plume
Red as the rising sun with heathen blood,
And seeing me, with a great voice he cried,
'They are broken, they are broken!' for the King,
However mild he seems at home, nor cares   310
For triumph in our mimic wars, the jousts—
For if his own knight casts him down, he laughs,
Saying his knights are better men than he—
Yet in this heathen war the fire of God
Fills him: I never saw his like; there lives   315
No greater leader."

            While he utter'd this,
Low to her own heart said the lily maid,
"Save your great self, fair lord"; and when he fell
From talk of war to traits of pleasantry—
Being mirthful he, but in a stately kind—   320
She still took note that when the living smile
Died from his lips, across him came a cloud
Of melancholy severe, from which again,
Whenever in her hovering to and fro
The lily maid had striven to make him cheer,   325
There brake a sudden-beaming tenderness
Of manners and of nature: and she thought
That all was nature, all, perchance, for her.
And all night long his face before her lived,
As when a painter, poring on a face,   330

Divinely thro' all hindrance finds the man
Behind it, and so paints him that his face,
The shape and color of a mind and life,
Lives for his children, ever at its best
And fullest; so the face before her lived, 335
Dark-splendid, speaking in the silence, full
Of noble things, and held her from her sleep,
Till rathe she rose, half-cheated in the thought
She needs must bid farewell to sweet Lavaine.
First as in fear, step after step, she stole 340
Down the long tower-stairs, hesitating:
Anon, she heard Sir Lancelot cry in the court,
"This shield, my friend, where is it?" and Lavaine
Past inward, as she came from out the tower.
There to his proud horse Lancelot turn'd, and smooth'd
The glossy shoulder, humming to himself. 346
Half-envious of the flattering hand, she drew
Nearer and stood. He look'd, and, more amazed
Than if seven men had set upon him, saw
The maiden standing in the dewy light. 350
He had not dream'd she was so beautiful.
Then came on him a sort of sacred fear,
For silent, tho' he greeted her, she stood
Rapt on his face as if it were a god's.
Suddenly flash'd on her a wild desire 355
That he should wear her favor at the tilt.
She braved a riotous heart in asking for it.
"Fair lord, whose name I know not—noble it is,
I well believe, the noblest—will you wear
My favor at this tourney?" "Nay," said he, 360

"Fair lady, since I never yet have worn
Favor of any lady in the lists.
Such is my wont, as those who know me know."
"Yea, so," she answer'd; "then in wearing mine
Needs must be lesser likelihood, noble lord,   365
That those who know should know you."   And he turn'd
Her counsel up and down within his mind,
And found it true, and answer'd: "True, my child.
Well, I will wear it: fetch it out to me:
What is it?" and she told him, "A red sleeve   370
Broider'd with pearls," and brought it: then he bound
Her token on his helmet, with a smile
Saying, "I never yet have done so much
For any maiden living," and the blood
Sprang to her face and fill'd her with delight;   375
But left her all the paler when Lavaine
Returning brought the yet-unblazon'd shield,
His brother's; which he gave to Lancelot,
Who parted with his own to fair Elaine:
"Do me this grace, my child, to have my shield   380
In keeping till I come."   "A grace to me,"
She answer'd, "twice to-day.   I am your squire!"
Whereat Lavaine said laughing: "Lily maid,
For fear our people call you lily maid
In earnest, let me bring your color back;   385
Once, twice, and thrice: now get you hence to bed":
So kiss'd her, and Sir Lancelot his own hand,
And thus they moved away: she staid a minute,
Then made a sudden step to the gate, and there—

Her bright hair blown about the serious face 390
Yet rosy-kindled with her brother's kiss—
Paused by the gateway, standing near the shield
In silence, while she watch'd their arms far-off
Sparkle, until they dipt below the downs.
Then to her tower she climb'd, and took the shield,
There kept it, and so lived in fantasy. 396

Meanwhile the new companions past away
Far o'er the long backs of the bushless downs,
To where Sir Lancelot knew there lived a knight
Not far from Camelot, now for forty years 400
A hermit, who had pray'd, labor'd and pray'd,
And ever laboring had scoop'd himself
In the white rock a chapel and a hall
On massive columns, like a shore-cliff cave,
And cells and chambers: all were fair and dry; 405
The green light from the meadows underneath
Struck up and lived along the milky roofs;
And in the meadows tremulous aspen-trees
And poplars made a noise of falling showers.
And thither wending there that night they bode. 410

But when the next day broke from underground,
And shot red fire and shadows thro' the cave,
They rose, heard mass, broke fast, and rode away.
Then Lancelot saying, "Hear, but hold my name
Hidden, you ride with Lancelot of the Lake," 415
Abash'd Lavaine, whose instant reverence,
Dearer to true young hearts than their own praise,

But left him leave to stammer, "Is it indeed?"
And after muttering, "The great Lancelot,"
At last he got his breath and answer'd: "One,   42◦
One have I seen—that other, our liege lord,
The dread Pendragon, Britain's King of kings,
Of whom the people talk mysteriously,
He will be there—then were I stricken blind
That minute, I might say that I had seen."   42◦

So spake Lavaine, and when they reach'd the lists
By Camelot in the meadow, let his eyes
Run thro' the peopled gallery which half round
Lay like a rainbow fallen upon the grass,
Until they found the clear-faced King, who sat   43◦
Robed in red samite, easily to be known,
Since to his crown the golden dragon clung,
And down his robe the dragon writhed in gold,
And from the carven-work behind him crept
Two dragons gilded, sloping down to make   435
Arms for his chair, while all the rest of them
Thro' knots and loops and folds innumerable
Fled ever thro' the woodwork, till they found
The new design wherein they lost themselves,
Yet with all ease, so tender was the work: 44◦
And, in the costly canopy o'er him set,
Blazed the last diamond of the nameless king.

Then Lancelot answer'd young Lavaine and said:
"Me you call great: mine is the firmer seat,
The truer lance: but there is many a youth   445

Now crescent, who will come to all I am
And overcome it; and in me there dwells
No greatness, save it be some far-off touch
Of greatness to know well I am not great:
There is the man." And Lavaine gaped upon him   450
As on a thing miraculous, and anon
The trumpets blew; and then did either side,
They that assail'd, and they that held the lists,
Set lance in rest, strike spur, suddenly move,
Meet in the midst, and there so furiously   455
Shock that a man far-off might well perceive,
If any man that day were left afield,
The hard earth shake, and a low thunder of arms.
And Lancelot bode a little, till he saw
Which were the weaker; then he hurl'd into it   460
Against the stronger: little need to speak
Of Lancelot in his glory! King, duke, earl,
Count, baron—whom he smote, he overthrew.

But in the field were Lancelot's kith and kin,
Ranged with the Table Round that held the lists,   465
Strong men, and wrathful that a stranger knight
Should do and almost overdo the deeds
Of Lancelot; and one said to the other, "Lo!
What is he? I do not mean the force alone—
The grace and versatility of the man!   470
Is it not Lancelot?" "When has Lancelot worn
Favor of any lady in the lists?
Not such his wont, as we that know him know."
"How then? who then?" a fury seized them all,

A fiery family passion for the name   475
Of Lancelot, and a glory one with theirs.
They couch'd their spears and prick'd their steeds, and
        thus,
Their plumes driven backward by the wind they made
In moving, all together down upon him
Bare, as a wild wave in the wide North Sea,   480
Green-glimmering toward the summit, bears, with all
Its stormy crests that smoke against the skies,
Down on a bark, and overbears the bark
And him that helms it; so they overbore
Sir Lancelot and his charger, and a spear   485
Down-glancing lamed the charger, and a spear
Prick'd sharply his own cuirass, and the head
Pierced thro' his side, and there snapt and remain'd.

Then Sir Lavaine did well and worshipfully:
He bore a knight of old repute to the earth,   490
And brought his horse to Lancelot where he lay.
He up the side, sweating with agony, got,
But thought to do while he might yet endure,
And being lustily holpen by the rest,
His party,—tho' it seem'd half-miracle   495
To those he fought with,—drave his kith and kin,
And all the Table Round that held the lists,
Back to the barrier; then the trumpets blew
Proclaiming his the prize who wore the sleeve
Of scarlet and the pearls; and all the knights,   500
His party, cried, "Advance and take thy prize
The diamond"; but he answer'd: "Diamond me

No diamonds! for God's love, a little air!
Prize me no prizes, for my prize is death!
Hence will I, and I charge you, follow me not."   505

He spoke, and vanish'd suddenly from the field
With young Lavaine into the poplar grove.
There from his charger down he slid, and sat,
Gasping to Sir Lavaine, "Draw the lance-head."
"Ah, my sweet lord Sir Lancelot," said Lavaine,   510
"I dread me, if I draw it, you will die."
But he, "I die already with it: draw—
Draw,"—and Lavaine drew, and Sir Lancelot gave
A marvellous great shriek and ghastly groan,
And half his blood burst forth, and down he sank   515
For the pure pain, and wholly swoon'd away.
Then came the hermit out and bare him in,
There stanch'd his wound; and there, in daily doubt
Whether to live or die, for many a week
Hid from the wild world's rumor by the grove   520
Of poplars with their noise of falling showers,
And ever-tremulous aspen-trees, he lay.

But on that day when Lancelot fled the lists,
His party, knights of utmost North and West,
Lords of waste marshes, kings of desolate isles,   525
Came round their great Pendragon, saying to him,
"Lo, Sire, our knight, thro' whom we won the day,
Hath gone sore wounded, and hath left his prize
Untaken, crying that his prize is death."
"Heaven hinder," said the King, "that such an one,   530

So great a knight as we have seen to-day—
He seem'd to me another Lancelot—
Yea, twenty times I thought him Lancelot—
He must not pass uncared for. Wherefore rise,
O Gawain, and ride forth and find the knight.   535
Wounded and wearied, needs must he be near.
I charge you that you get at once to horse.
And, knights and kings, there breathes not one of
      you
Will deem this prize of ours is rashly given:
His prowess was too wondrous. We will do him   540
No customary honor: since the knight
Came not to us, of us to claim the prize,
Ourselves will send it after. Rise and take
This diamond, and deliver it, and return,
And bring us where he is, and how he fares,   545
And cease not from your quest until ye find."

So saying, from the carven flower above,
To which it made a restless heart, he took
And gave the diamond: then from where he sat
At Arthur's right, with smiling face arose,   550
With smiling face and frowning heart, a prince
In the mid might and flourish of his May,
Gawain, surnamed the Courteous, fair and strong,
And after Lancelot, Tristram, and Geriant,
And Gareth, a good knight, but therewithal   555
Sir Modred's brother, and the child of Lot,
Nor often loyal to his word, and now
Wroth that the King's command to sally forth

In quest of whom he knew not, made him leave
The banquet and concourse of knights and kings.   560

    So all in wrath he got to horse and went;
While Arthur to the banquet, dark in mood,
Past, thinking, "Is it Lancelot who hath come
Despite the wound he spake of, all for gain
Of glory, and hath added wound to wound,   565
And ridden away to die?" So fear'd the King,
And, after two days' tarriance there, return'd.
Then when he saw the Queen, embracing ask'd,
"Love, are you yet so sick?" "Nay, lord," she
            said.
"And where is Lancelot?" Then the Queen amazed, 570
"Was he not with you? won he not your prize?"
"Nay, but one like him." "Why, that like was
            he."
And when the King demanded how she knew,
Said: "Lord, no sooner had ye parted from us
Than Lancelot told me of a common talk   575
That men went down before his spear at a touch,
But knowing he was Lancelot; his great name
Conquer'd; and therefore would he hide his name
From all men, even the King, and to this end
Had made the pretext of a hindering wound,   580
That he might joust unknown of all, and learn
If his old prowess were in aught decay'd;
And added, 'Our true Arthur, when he learns,
Will well allow my pretext, as for gain
Of purer glory.'"

　　　　　　Then replied the King:　　　585
"Far lovelier in our Lancelot had it been,
In lieu of idly dallying with the truth,
To have trusted me as he hath trusted thee.
Surely his King and most familiar friend
Might well have kept his secret. True, indeed,　　590
Albeit I know my knights fantastical,
So fine a fear in our large Lancelot
Must needs have moved my laughter: now re-
　　　mains
But little cause for laughter: his own kin—
Ill news, my Queen, for all who love him, this!—　　595
His kith and kin, not knowing, set upon him;
So that he went sore wounded from the field.
Yet good news too; for goodly hopes are mine
That Lancelot is no more a lonely heart.
He wore, against his wont, upon his helm　　600
A sleeve of scarlet, broider'd with great pearls,
Some gentle maiden's gift."

　　　　　　　　　"Yea, lord," she said,
"Thy hopes are mine," and saying that, she choked,
And sharply turn'd about to hide her face,
Past to her chamber, and there flung herself　　605
Down on the great King's couch, and writhed upon
　　　it,
And clench'd her fingers till they bit the palm,
And shriek'd out "Traitor!" to the unhearing wall,
Then flash'd into wild tears, and rose again,
And moved about her palace, proud and pale.　　610

Gawain the while thro' all the region round
Rode with his diamond, wearied of the quest,
Touch'd at all points except the poplar grove,
And came at last, tho' late, to Astolat;
Whom glittering in enamell'd arms the maid   615
Glanced at, and cried, "What news from Camelot, lord?
What of the knight with the red sleeve?" "He won."
"I knew it," she said. "But parted from the jousts
Hurt in the side;" whereat she caught her breath;
Thro' her own side she felt the sharp lance go;   620
Thereon she smote her hand; wellnigh she swoon'd:
And, while he gazed wonderingly at her, came
The Lord of Astolat out, to whom the prince
Reported who he was, and on what quest
Sent, that he bore the prize and could not find   625
The victor, but had ridden a random round
To seek him, and had wearied of the search.
To whom the Lord of Astolat: "Bide with us,
And ride no more at random, noble prince!
Here was the knight, and here he left a shield;   630
This will he send or come for: furthermore
Our son is with him; we shall hear anon,
Needs must we hear." To this the courteous prince
Accorded with his wonted courtesy,
Courtesy with a touch of traitor in it,   635
And staid; and cast his eyes on fair Elaine;
Where could be found face daintier? then her shape
From forehead down to foot, perfect—again
From foot to forehead exquisitely turn'd:
"Well—if I bide, lo! this wild flower for me!"   640

And oft they met among the garden yews,
And there he set himself to play upon her
With sallying wit, free flashes from a height
Above her, graces of the court, and songs,
Sighs, and low smiles, and golden eloquence   645
And amorous adulation, till the maid
Rebell'd against it, saying to him: "Prince,
O loyal nephew of our noble King,
Why ask you not to see the shield he left,
Whence you might learn his name?   Why slight your
    King,   650
And lose the quest he sent you on, and prove
No surer than our falcon yesterday,
Who lost the hern we slipt her at, and went
To all the winds?"   "Nay, by mine head," said he,
"I lose it, as we lose the lark in heaven,   655
O damsel, in the light of your blue eyes;
But an ye will it let me see the shield."
And when the shield was brought, and Gawain saw
Sir Lancelot's azure lions, crown'd with gold,
Ramp in the field, he smote his thigh, and mock'd: 660
"Right was the King! our Lancelot! that true man!"
"And right was I," she answer'd merrily, "I,
Who dream'd my knight the greatest knight of all."
"And if *I* dream'd," said Gawain, "that you love
This greatest knight, your pardon! lo, ye know it!   665
Speak therefore: shall I waste myself in vain?"
Full simple was her answer: "What know I?
My brethren have been all my fellowship;
And I, when often they have talk'd of love,

Wish'd it had been my mother, for they talk'd,   670
Meseem'd, of what they knew not; so myself—
I know not if I know what true love is,
But if I know, then, if I love not him,
I know there is none other I can love."
"Yea, by God's death," said he, "ye love him well,
But would not, knew ye what all others know,   676
And whom he loves."   "So be it," cried Elaine,
And lifted her fair face and moved away:
But he pursued her, calling, "Stay a little!
One golden minute's grace! he wore your sleeve: 680
Would he break faith with one I may not name?
Must our true man change like a leaf at last?
Nay—like enow: why then, far be it from me
To cross our mighty Lancelot in his loves!
And, damsel, for I deem you know full well   685
Where your great knight is hidden, let me leave
My quest with you; the diamond also: here!
For if you love, it will be sweet to give it;
And if he love, it will be sweet to have it
From your own hand; and whether he love or not,   690
A diamond is a diamond.   Fare you well
A thousand times!—a thousand times farewell!
Yet, if he love, and his love hold, we two
May meet at court hereafter: there, I think,
So ye will learn the courtesies of the court,   695
We two shall know each other."

                              Then he gave,
And slightly kiss'd the hand to which he gave,

The diamond, and all wearied of the quest
Leapt on his horse, and carolling as he went
A true-love ballad, lightly rode away.   700

   Thence to the court he past; there told the King
What the King knew, "Sir Lancelot is the knight."
And added, "Sire, my liege, so much I learnt;
But fail'd to find him, tho' I rode all round
The region: but I lighted on the maid   705
Whose sleeve he wore; she loves him; and to her,
Deeming our courtesy is the truest law,
I gave the diamond: she will render it;
For by mine head she knows his hiding-place."

   The seldom-frowning King frown'd, and replied,   710
"Too courteous truly! ye shall go no more
On quest of mine, seeing that ye forget
Obedience is the courtesy due to kings."

   He spake and parted. Wroth, but all in awe,
For twenty strokes of the blood, without a word,   715
Linger'd that other, staring after him;
Then shook his hair, strode off, and buzz'd abroad
About the maid of Astolat, and her love.
All ears were prick'd at once, all tongues were loosed:
"The maid of Astolat loves Sir Lancelot,   720
Sir Lancelot loves the maid of Astolat."
Some read the King's face, some the Queen's, and all
Had marvel what the maid might be, but most
Predoom'd her as unworthy. One old dame

Came suddenly on the Queen with the sharp news.   725
She, that had heard the noise of it before,
But sorrowing Lancelot should have stoop'd so low,
Marr'd her friend's aim with pale tranquillity.
So ran the tale like fire about the court,
Fire in dry stubble a nine-days' wonder flared: 730
Till even the knights at banquet twice or thrice
Forgot to drink to Lancelot and the Queen,
And pledging Lancelot and the lily maid
Smiled at each other, while the Queen, who sat
With lips severely placid, felt the knot   735
Climb in her throat, and with her feet unseen
Crush'd the wild passion out against the floor
Beneath the banquet, where the meats became
As wormwood and she hated all who pledged.

But far away the maid in Astolat,   740
Her guiltless rival, she that ever kept
The one-day-seen Sir Lancelot in her heart,
Crept to her father, while he mused alone,
Sat on his knee, stroked his gray face and said:
"Father, you call me wilful, and the fault   745
Is yours who let me have my will, and now,
Sweet father, will you let me lose my wits?"
"Nay," said he, "surely." "Wherefore, let me hence,"
She answer'd, "and find out our dear Lavaine."
"Ye will not lose your wits for dear Lavaine: 750
Bide," answer'd he: "we needs must hear anon
Of him, and of that other." "Ay," she said,
"And of that other, for I needs must hence

And find that other, wherso'er he be,
And with mine own hand give his diamond to him,   755
Lest I be found as faithless in the quest
As yon proud prince who left the quest to me.
Sweet father, I behold him in my dreams
Gaunt as it were the skeleton of himself,
Death-pale, for the lack of gentle maiden's aid.   760
The gentler-born the maiden, the more bound,
My father, to be sweet and serviceable
To noble knights in sickness, as ye know,
When these have worn their tokens: let me hence,
I pray you." Then her father nodding said: 765
"Ay, ay, the diamond: wit ye well, my child,
Right fain were I to learn this knight were whole,
Being our greatest: yea, and you must give it—
And sure I think this fruit is hung too high
For any mouth to gape for save a queen's—   770
Nay, I mean nothing: so then, get you gone,
Being so very wilful you must go."

Lightly, her suit allow'd, she slipt away,
And while she made her ready for her ride
Her father's latest word humm'd in her ear,   775
"Being so very wilful you must go,"
And changed itself and echo'd in her heart,
"Being so very wilful you must die."
But she was happy enough and shook it off,
As we shake off the bee that buzzes at us;   780
And in her heart she answer'd it and said,
"What matter, so I help him back to life?"

Then far away with good Sir Torre for guide
Rode o'er the long backs of the bushless downs
To Camelot, and before the city-gates   785
Came on her brother with a happy face
Making a roan horse caper and curvet
For pleasure all about a field of flowers;
Whom when she saw, "Lavaine," she cried, "Lavaine,
How fares my lord Sir Lancelot?" He amazed,   790
"Torre and Elaine! why here? Sir Lancelot!
How know ye my lord's name is Lancelot?"
But when the maid had told him all her tale,
Then turn'd Sir Torre, and being in his moods
Left them, and under the strange-statued gate,   795
Where Arthur's wars were render'd mystically,
Past up the still rich city to his kin,
His own far blood, which dwelt at Camelot;
And her, Lavaine across the poplar grove
Led to the caves: there first she saw the casque   800
Of Lancelot on the wall: her scarlet sleeve,
Tho' carved and cut, and half the pearls away,
Stream'd from it still; and in her heart she laugh'd,
Because he had not loosed it from his helm,
But meant once more perchance to tourney in it.   805
And when they gain'd the cell wherein he slept,
His battle-writhen arms and mighty hands
Lay naked on the wolf-skin, and a dream
Of dragging down his enemy made them move.
Then she that saw him lying unsleek, unshorn,   810
Gaunt as it were the skeleton of himself,
Utter'd a little tender dolorous cry.

The sound not wonted in a place so still
Woke the sick knight, and while he roll'd his eyes
Yet blank from sleep, she started to him, saying,   815
"Your prize the diamond sent you by the King."
His eyes glisten'd: she fancied, "Is it for me?"
And when the maid had told him all the tale
Of king and prince, the diamond sent, the quest
Assign'd to her not worthy of it, she knelt   820
Full lowly by the corners of his bed,
And laid the diamond in his open hand.
Her face was near, and as we kiss the child
That does the task assign'd, he kiss'd her face.
At once she slipt like water to the floor.   825
"Alas," he said, "your ride hath wearied you.
Rest must you have." "No rest for me," she said;
"Nay, for near you, fair lord, I am at rest."
What might she mean by that? his large black
        eyes,
Yet larger thro' his leanness, dwelt upon her,   830
Till all her heart's sad secret blazed itself
In the heart's colors on her simple face;
And Lancelot look'd and was perplext in mind
And being weak in body said no more,
But did not love the color; woman's love,   835
Save one, he not regarded, and so turn'd
Sighing, and feign'd a sleep until he slept.

Then rose Elaine and glided thro' the fields,
And past beneath the weirdly-sculptured gates
Far up the dim rich city to her kin;   840

There bode the night: but woke with dawn, and past
Down thro' the dim rich city to the fields,
Thence to the cave. So day by day she past
In either twilight ghost-like to and fro
Gliding, and every day she tended him,   845
And likewise many a night; and Lancelot
Would, tho' he call'd his wound a little hurt
Whereof he should be quickly whole, at times
Brain-feverous in his heat and agony, seem
Uncourteous, even he: but the meek maid   850
Sweetly forbore him ever, being to him
Meeker than any child to a rough nurse,
Milder than any mother to a sick child,
And never woman yet, since man's first fall,
Did kindlier unto man, but her deep love   855
Upbore her; till the hermit, skill'd in all
The simples and the science of that time,
Told him that her fine care had saved his life.
And the sick man forgot her simple blush,
Would call her friend and sister, sweet Elaine,   860
Would listen for her coming and regret
Her parting step, and held her tenderly,
And loved her with all love except the love
Of man and woman when they love their best,
Closest and sweetest, and had died the death   865
In any knightly fashion for her sake.
And peradventure had he seen her first
She might have made this and that other world
Another world for the sick man; but now
The shackles of an old love straiten'd him,   870

His honor rooted in dishonor stood,
And faith unfaithful kept him falsely true.

　　Yet the great knight in his mid-sickness made
Full many a holy vow and pure resolve.
These, as but born of sickness, could not live;　　875
For when the blood ran lustier in him again,
Full often the bright image of one face,
Making a treacherous quiet in his heart,
Dispersed his resolution like a cloud.
Then if the maiden, while that ghostly grace　　880
Beam'd on his fancy, spoke, he answer'd not,
Or short and coldly, and she knew right well
What the rough sickness meant, but what this
　　　　meant
She knew not, and the sorrow dimm'd her sight,
And drave her ere time across the fields　　885
Far into the rich city, where alone
She murmur'd, "Vain, in vain: it cannot be.
He will not love me: how then? must I die?"
Then as a little helpless innocent bird,
That has but one plain passage of few notes,　　890
Will sing the simple passage o'er and o'er
For all an April morning, till the ear
Wearies to hear it, so the simple maid
Went half the night repeating, "Must I die?"
And now to right she turn'd, and now to left,　　895
And found no ease in turning or in rest;
And "Him or death," she mutter'd, "death or him,"
Again and like a burthen, "Him or death."

But when Sir Lancelot's deadly hurt was whole,
To Astolat returning rode the three.   900
There morn by morn, arraying her sweet self
In that wherein she deem'd she look'd her best,
She came before Sir Lancelot, for she thought,
"If I be loved, these are my festal robes,
If not, the victim's flowers before he fall."   905
And Lancelot ever prest upon the maid
That she should ask some goodly gift of him
For her own self or hers: "and do not shun
To speak the wish most near to your true heart;
Such service have ye done me that I make   910
My will of yours, and prince and lord am I
In mine own land, and what I will I can."
Then like a ghost she lifted up her face,
But like a ghost without the power to speak.
And Lancelot saw that she withheld her wish,   915
And bode among them yet a little space
Till he should learn it; and one morn it chanced
He found her in among the garden yews,
And said, "Delay no longer, speak your wish,
Seeing I go to-day:" then out she brake: 920
"Going? and we shall never see you more.
And I must die for want of one bold word."
"Speak: that I live to hear," he said, "is yours."
Then suddenly and passionately she spoke:
"I have gone mad. I love you: let me die."   925
"Ah, sister," answer'd Lancelot, "what is this?"
And innocently extending her white arms,
"Your love," she said, "your love—to be your wife."

And Lancelot answer'd, "Had I chosen to wed,
I had been wedded earlier, sweet Elaine;   930
But now there never will be wife of mine."
"No, no," she cried, "I care not to be wife,
But to be with you still, to see your face,
To serve you, and to follow you thro' the world."
And Lancelot answer'd: "Nay, the world, the world,
All ear and eye, with such a stupid heart   936
To interpret ear and eye, and such a tongue
To blare its own interpretation—nay,
Full ill then should I quit your brother's love,
And your good father's kindness."   And she said,   940
"Not to be with you, not to see your face—
Alas for me then, my good days are done!"
"Nay, noble maid," he answer'd, "ten times nay!
This is not love, but love's first flash in youth,
Most common: yea, I know it of mine own self;   945
And you yourself will smile at your own self
Hereafter, when you yield your flower of life
To one more fitly yours, not thrice your age.
And then will I, for true you are and sweet
Beyond mine old belief in womanhood,   950
More specially should your good knight be poor,
Endow you with broad land and territory
Even to the half my realm beyond the seas,
So that would make you happy: furthermore,
Even to the death, as tho' ye were my blood,   955
In all your quarrels will I be your knight.
This will I do, dear damsel, for your sake,
And more than this I cannot."

While he spoke
She neither blush'd nor shook, but deathly-pale
Stood grasping what was nearest, then replied,   960
"Of all this will I nothing"; and so fell,
And thus they bore her swooning to her tower.

Then spake, to whom thro' those black walls of yew
Their talk had pierced, her father: "Ay, a flash,
I fear me, that will strike my blossom dead.   965
Too courteous are ye, fair Lord Lancelot.
I pray you, use some rough discourtesy
To blunt or break her passion."

Lancelot said,
"That were against me: what I can I will;"
And there that day remain'd, and toward even   970
Sent for his shield: full meekly rose the maid,
Stript off the case, and gave the naked shield;
Then, when she heard his horse upon the stones,
Unclasping flung the casement back, and look'd
Down on his helm, from which her sleeve had gone.
And Lancelot knew the little clinking sound;   976
And she by tact of love was well aware
That Lancelot knew that she was looking at him.
And yet he glanced not up, nor waved his hand,
Nor bade farewell, but sadly rode away.   980
This was the one discourtesy that he used.

So in her tower alone the maiden sat:
His very shield was gone; only the case,

Her own poor work, her empty labor, left.
But still she heard him, still his picture form'd   985
And grew between her and the pictured wall.
Then came her father, saying in low tones,
"Have comfort," whom she greeted quietly.
Then came her brethren saying, "Peace to thee,
Sweet sister," whom she answer'd with all calm.   990
But when they left her to herself again,
Death, like a friend's voice from a distant field
Approaching thro' the darkness, call'd; the owls
Wailing had power upon her, and she mixt
Her fancies with the sallow-rifted glooms   995
Of evening and the moanings of the wind.

And in those days she made a little song,
And call'd her song "The Song of Love and Death,"
And sang it: sweetly could she make and sing.

"Sweet is true love tho' given in vain, in vain;   1000
And sweet is death who puts an end to pain:
I know not which is sweeter, no, not I.

"Love, art thou sweet? then bitter death must
    be:
Love, thou art bitter; sweet is death to me.
O Love, if death be sweeter, let me die.   1005

"Sweet love, that seems not made to fade away;
Sweet death, that seems to make us loveless clay;
I know not which is sweeter, no, not I.

"I fain would follow love, if that could be;
I needs must follow death, who calls for me;   1010
Call and I follow, I follow! let me die."

High with the last line scaled her voice, and this,
All in a fiery dawning wild with wind
That shook her tower, the brothers heard, and
      thought
With shuddering, "Hark the Phantom of the house 1015
That ever shrieks before a death," and call'd
The father, and all three in hurry and fear
Ran to her, and lo! the blood-red light of dawn
Flared on her face, she shrilling, "Let me die!"

As when we dwell upon a word we know,   1020
Repeating, till the word we know so well
Becomes a wonder, and we know not why
So dwelt the father on her face, and thought,
"Is this Elaine?" till back the maiden fell,
Then gave a languid hand to each, and lay,   1025
Speaking a still good-morrow with her eyes.
At last she said: "Sweet brothers, yesternight
I seem'd a curious little maid again,
As happy as when we dwelt among the woods,
And when ye used to take me with the flood   1030
Up the great river in the boatman's boat.
Only ye would not pass beyond the cape
That has the poplar on it: there ye fixt
Your limit, oft returning with the tide.
And yet I cried because ye would not pass   1035

Beyond it, and far up the shining flood
Until we found the palace of the King.
And yet ye would not; but this night I dream'd
That I was all alone upon the flood,
And then I said, 'Now shall I have my will:'   1040
And there I woke, but still the wish remain'd.
So let me hence that I may pass at last
Beyond the poplar and far up the flood,
Until I find the palace of the King.
There will I enter in among them all,   1045
And no man there will dare to mock at me;
But there the fine Gawain will wonder at me,
And there the great Sir Lancelot muse at me;
Gawain, who bade a thousand farewells to me,
Lancelot, who coldly went, nor bade me one: 1050
And there the King will know me and my love,
And there the Queen herself will pity me,
And all the gentle court will welcome me,
And after my long voyage I shall rest!"

   "Peace," said her father, "O my child, ye seem   1055
Light-headed, for what force is yours to go
So far, being sick? and wherefore would ye look
On this proud fellow again, who scorns us all?"

   Then the rough Torre began to heave and move,
And bluster into stormy sobs and say: 1060
"I never loved him: an I meet with him,
I care not howsoever great he be,
Then will I strike at him and strike him down;

Give me good fortune, I will strike him dead,
For this discomfort he hath done the house." 1065

To whom the gentle sister made reply:
'Fret not yourself, dear brother, nor be wroth,
Seeing it is no more Sir Lancelot's fault
Not to love me than it is mine to love
Him of all men who seems to me the highest." 1070

"Highest?" the father answer'd, echoing "highest?"—
He meant to break the passion in her—"nay,
Daughter, I know not what you call the highest;
But this I know, for all the people know it,
He loves the Queen, and in an open shame: 1075
And she returns his love in open shame;
If this be high, what is it to be low?"

Then spake the lily maid of Astolat:
'Sweet father, all too faint and sick am I
For anger: these are slanders; never yet 1080
Was noble man but made ignoble talk.
He makes no friend who never made a foe.
But now it is my glory to have loved
One peerless, without stain: so let me pass,
My father, howsoe'er I seem to you, 1085
Not all unhappy, having loved God's best
And greatest, tho' my love had no return:
Yet, seeing you desire your child to live,
Thanks, but you work against your own desire;
For if I could believe the things you say 1090

I should but die the sooner; wherefore cease,
Sweet father, and bid call the ghostly man
Hither, and let me shrive me clean and die."

So when the ghostly man had come and gone,
She, with a face bright as for sin forgiven,   1095
Besought Lavaine to write as she devised
A letter, word for word; and when he ask'd,
"Is it for Lancelot, is it for my dear lord?
Then will I bear it gladly"; she replied,
"For Lancelot and the Queen and all the world,   1100
But I myself must bear it."   Then he wrote
The letter she devised; which being writ
And folded, "O sweet father, tender and true,
Deny me not," she said—"ye never yet
Denied my fancies—this, however strange,   1105
My latest: lay the letter in my hand
A little ere I die, and close the hand
Upon it; I shall guard it even in death.
And when the heat has gone from out my heart,
Then take the little bed on which I died   1110
For Lancelot's love, and deck it like the Queen's
For richness, and me also like the Queen
In all I have of rich, and lay me on it.
And let there be prepared a chariot-bier
To take me to the river, and a barge   1115
Be ready on the river, clothed in black.
I go in state to court, to meet the Queen.
There surely I shall speak for mine own self,
And none of you can speak for me so well.

And therefore let our dumb old man alone   1120
Go with me; he can steer and row, and he
Will guide me to that palace, to the doors."

    She ceased: her father promised; whereupon
She grew so cheerful that they deem'd her death
Was rather in the fantasy than the blood.   1125
But ten slow mornings past, and on the eleventh
Her father laid the letter in her hand,
And closed the hand upon it, and she died.
So that day there was dole in Astolat.

    But when the next sun brake from underground,   1130
Then, those two brethren slowly with bent brows
Accompanying, the sad chariot-bier
Past like a shadow thro' the field, that shone
Full-summer, to that stream whereon the barge,
Pall'd all its length in blackest samite, lay.   1135
There sat the lifelong creature of the house,
Loyal, the dumb old servitor, on deck,
Winking his eyes, and twisted all his face.
So those two brethren from the chariot took
And on the black decks laid her in her bed,   1140
Set in her hand a lily, o'er her hung
The silken case with braided blazonings,
And kiss'd her quiet brows, and saying to her,
"Sister, farewell forever," and again,
"Farewell, sweet sister," parted all in tears.   1145
Then rose the dumb old servitor, and the dead,
Oar'd by the dumb, went upward with the flood—

In her right hand the lily, in her left
The letter—all her bright hair streaming down—
And all the coverlid was cloth of gold   1150
Drawn to her waist, and she herself in white
All but her face, and that clear-featured face
Was lovely, for she did not seem as dead,
But fast asleep, and lay as tho' she smiled.

That day Sir Lancelot at the palace craved   1155
Audience of Guinevere, to give at last
The price of half a realm, his costly gift,
Hard-won and hardly won with bruise and blow,
With deaths of others, and almost his own,
The nine-years-fought-for diamonds; for he saw 1160
One of her house, and sent him to the Queen
Bearing his wish, whereto the Queen agreed
With such and so unmoved a majesty
She might have seem'd her statue, but that he,
Low-drooping till he wellnigh kiss'd her feet   1165
For loyal awe, saw with a sidelong eye
The shadow of some piece of pointed lace,
In the Queen's shadow, vibrate on the walls,
And parted, laughing in his courtly heart.

All in an oriel on the summer side,   1170
Vine-clad, of Arthur's palace toward the stream,
They met, and Lancelot kneeling utter'd: "Queen,
Lady, my liege, in whom I have my joy,
Take, what I had not won except for you,
These jewels, and make me happy, making them   1175

An armlet for the roundest arm on earth,
Or necklace for a neck to which the swan's
Is tawnier than her cygnet's: these are words;
Your beauty is your beauty, and I sin
In speaking, yet O, grant my worship of it   1180
Words, as we grant grief tears. Such sin in words
Perchance, we both can pardon; but, my Queen,
I hear of rumors flying thro' your court.
Our bond, as not the bond of man and wife,
Should have in it an absoluter trust   1185
To make up that defect: let rumors be:
When did not rumors fly? these, as I trust
That you trust me in your own nobleness,
I may not well believe that you believe."

    While thus he spoke, half turn'd away, the Queen 1190
Brake from the vast oriel-embowering vine
Leaf after leaf, and tore, and cast them off,
Till all the place whereon she stood was green;
Then, when he ceased, in one cold passive hand
Received at once and laid aside the gems   1195
There on a table near her, and replied:

    "It may be I am quicker of belief
Than you believe me, Lancelot of the Lake.
Our bond is not the bond of man and wife.
This good is in it, whatsoe'er of ill,   1200
It can be broken easier. I for you
This many a year have done despite and wrong
To one whom ever in my heart of hearts

I did acknowledge nobler. What are these?
Diamonds for me! they had been thrice their worth 1205
Being your gift, had you not lost your own.
To loyal hearts the value of all gifts
Must vary as the giver's. Not for me!
For her! for your new fancy. Only this
Grant me, I pray you: have your joys apart.　　　1210
I doubt not that, however changed, you keep
So much of what is graceful: and myself
Would shun to break those bounds of courtesy
In which as Arthur's Queen I move and rule;
So cannot speak my mind. An end to this!　　　1215
A strange one! yet I take it with Amen.
So pray you, add my diamonds to her pearls;
Deck her with these; tell her, she shines me down:
An armlet for an arm to which the Queen's
Is haggard, or a necklace for a neck　　　1220
O, as much fairer—as a faith once fair
Was richer than these diamonds—hers not mine—
Nay, by the mother of our Lord himself,
Or hers or mine, mine now to work my will—
She shall not have them."

　　　　　　　　　Saying which she seized, 1225
And, thro' the casement standing wide for heat,
Flung them, and down they flash'd, and smote the stream.
Then from the smitten surface flash'd, as it were,
Diamonds to meet them, and they past away.
Then while Sir Lancelot leant, in half disdain　　1230
At love, life, all things, on the window ledge,

Close underneath his eyes, and right across
Where these had fallen, slowly past the barge
Whereon the lily maid of Astolat
Lay smiling, like a star in blackest night.   1235

But the wild Queen, who saw not, burst away
To weep and wail in secret; and the barge,
On to the palace-doorway sliding, paused.
There two stood arm'd, and kept the door; to whom,
All up the marble stair, tier over tier,   1240
Were added mouths that gaped, and eyes that ask'd,
"What is it?" but that oarsman's haggard face,
As hard and still as is the face that men
Shape to their fancy's eye from broken rocks
On some cliff-side, appall'd them, and they said: 1245
"He is enchanted, cannot speak—and she,
Look how she sleeps—the Fairy Queen, so fair!
Yea, but how pale! what are they? flesh and blood?
Or come to take the King to Fairyland?
For some do hold our Arthur cannot die,   1250
But that he passes into Fairyland."

While thus they babbled of the King, the King
Came girt with knights: then turn'd the tongueless man
From the half-face to the full eye, and rose
And pointed to the damsel and the doors.   1255
So Arthur bade the meek Sir Percivale
And pure Sir Galahad to uplift the maid;
And reverently they bore her into hall.
Then came the fine Gawain and wonder'd at her,

And Lancelot later came and mused at her,   1260
And last the Queen herself, and pitied her;
But Arthur spied the letter in her hand,
Stoopt, took, brake seal, and read it; this was all:

"Most noble lord, Sir Lancelot of the Lake,
I, sometime call'd the maid of Astolat,   1265
Come, for you left me taking no farewell,
Hither, to take my last farewell of you.
I loved you, and my love had no return,
And therefore my true love has been my death.
And therefore to our Lady Guinevere,   1270
And to all other ladies, I make moan:
Pray for my soul, and yield me burial.
Pray for my soul thou too, Sir Lancelot,
As thou art a knight peerless."

                              Thus he read;
And ever in the reading lords and dames   1275
Wept, looking often from his face who read
To hers which lay so silent, and at times,
So touch'd were they, half-thinking that her lips
Who had devised the letter moved again.

Then freely spoke Sir Lancelot to them all: 1280
"My lord liege Arthur, and all ye that hear,
Know that for this most gentle maiden's death
Right heavy am I; for good she was and true,
But loved me with a love beyond all love
In women, whomsoever I have known.   1285

Yet to be loved makes not to love again;
Not at my years, however it hold in youth.
I swear by truth and knighthood that I gave
No cause, not willingly, for such a love.
To this I call my friends in testimony, 1290
Her brethren, and her father, who himself
Besought me to be plain and blunt, and use,
To break her passion, some discourtesy
Against my nature: what I could, I did.
I left her and I bade her no farewell; 1295
Tho', had I dreamt the damsel would have died,
I might have put my wits to some rough use,
And help'd her from herself."

      Then said the Queen—
Sea was her wrath, yet working after storm:
"Ye might at least have done her so much grace, 1300
Fair lord, as would have help'd her from her death."
He raised his head, their eyes met and hers fell,
He adding:

   "Queen, she would not be content
Save that I wedded her, which could not be.
Then might she follow me thro' the world, she ask'd;
It could not be. I told her that her love 1306
Was but the flash of youth, would darken down,
To rise hereafter in a stiller flame
Toward one more worthy of her—then would I,
More specially were he she wedded poor, 1310
Estate them with large land and territory
In mine own realm beyond the narrow seas,

To keep them in all joyance: more than this
I could not; this she would not, and she died."

He pausing, Arthur answer'd: "O my knight,   1315
It will be to thy worship, as my knight,
And mine, as head of all our Table Round,
To see that she be buried worshipfully."

So toward that shrine which then in all the realm
Was richest, Arthur leading, slowly went   1320
The marshall'd Order of their Table Round,
And Lancelot sad beyond his wont, to see
The maiden buried, not as one unknown,
Nor meanly, but with gorgeous obsequies,
And mass, and rolling music, like a queen.   1325
And when the knights had laid her comely head
Low in the dust of half-forgotten kings,
Then Arthur spake among them: "Let her tomb
Be costly, and her image thereupon,
And let the shield of Lancelot at her feet   1330
Be carven, and her lily in her hand.
And let the story of her dolorous voyage
For all true hearts be blazon'd on her tomb
In letters gold and azure!" which was wrought
Thereafter; but when now the lords and dames   1335
And people, from the high door streaming, brake
Disorderly, as homeward each, the Queen,
Who mark'd Sir Lancelot where he moved apart,
Drew near, and sigh'd in passing, "Lancelot,
Forgive me; mine was jealousy in love."   1340

He answer'd with his eyes upon the ground,
"That is love's curse; pass on, my Queen, forgiven."
But Arthur, who beheld his cloudy brows,
Approach'd him, and with full affection said:

"Lancelot, my Lancelot, thou in whom I have   1345
Most joy and most affiance, for I know
What thou hast been in battle by my side,
And many a time have watch'd thee at the tilt
Strike down the lusty and long practised knight
And let the younger and unskill'd go by   1350
To win his honor and to make his name,
And loved thy courtesies and thee, a man
Made to be loved; but now I would to God,
Seeing the homeless trouble in thine eyes,
Thou couldst have loved this maiden, shaped, it seems,
By God for thee alone, and from her face,   1356
If one may judge the living by the dead,
Delicately pure and marvellously fair,
Who might have brought thee, now a lonely man
Wifeless and heirless, noble issue, sons   1360
Born to the glory of thy name and fame,
My knight, the great Sir Lancelot of the Lake."

Then answer'd Lancelot: "Fair she was, my King,
Pure, as you ever wish your knights to be.
To doubt her fairness were to want an eye,   1365
To doubt her pureness were to want a heart—
Yea, to be loved, if what is worthy love
Could bind him, but free love will not be bound."

"Free love, so bound, were freest," said the King.
"Let love be free; free love is for the best: 1370
And, after heaven, on our dull side of death,
What should be best, if not so pure a love
Clothed in so pure a loveliness? yet thee
She fail'd to bind, tho' being, as I think,
Unbound as yet, and gentle, as I know."   1375

And Lancelot answer'd nothing, but he went,
And at the inrunning of a little brook
Sat by the river in a cove, and watch'd
The high reed wave, and lifted up his eyes
And saw the barge that brought her moving down,   1380
Far-off, a blot upon the stream, and said
Low in himself: "Ah, simple heart and sweet,
Ye loved me, damsel, surely with a love
Far tenderer than my Queen's. Pray for thy soul?
Ay, that will I. Farewell too—now at last—   1385
Farewell, fair lily. 'Jealousy in love?'
Not rather dead love's harsh heir, jealous pride?
Queen, if I grant the jealousy as of love,
May not your crescent fear for name and fame
Speak, as it waxes, of a love that wanes?   1390
Why did the King dwell on my name to me?
Mine own name shames me, seeming a reproach,
Lancelot, whom the Lady of the Lake
Caught from his mother's arms—the wondrous one
Who passes thro' the vision of the night—   1395
She chanted snatches of mysterious hymns
Heard on the winding waters, eve and morn

She kiss'd me saying, 'Thou art fair, my child,
As a king's son,' and often in her arms
She bare me, pacing on the dusky mere.   1400
Would she had drown'd me in it, where'er it be!
For what am I? what profits me my name
Of greatest knight? I fought for it, and have it:
Pleasure to have it, none; to lose it, pain:
Now grown a part of me: but what use in it?   1405
To make men worse by making my sin known?
Or sin seem less, the sinner seeming great?
Alas for Arthur's greatest knight, a man
Not after Arthur's heart! I needs must break
These bonds that so defame me: not without   1410
She wills it: would I, if she will'd it? nay,
Who knows? but if I would not, then may God,
I pray him, send a sudden angel down
To seize me by the hair and bear me far,
And fling me deep in that forgotten mere,   1415
Among the tumbled fragments of the hills."

So groan'd Sir Lancelot in remorseful pain,
Not knowing he should die a holy man.

THE HOLY GRAIL

In the complete *Idylls of the King*, as in this edition, "The Holy Grail" follows "Lancelot and Elaine." The search for the holy vessel from which Christ drank at the Last Supper is emblematic of the Christianity of the Dark and Middle Ages, which sought salvation in seclusion from humanity. Here, again, the interest centers in Lancelot, to whom the vessel with its healing powers becomes a scourge of fiery wrath. In contrast with the knights whose rash vows send them out to follow wandering fires, is King Arthur, who finds in his allotted task visions of exalting spiritual assurance.

"The Holy Grail" is a pure allegory of deep spiritual significance. The response of each of the prominent characters to the appeal of the quest, their varying experiences, and the poet's own comments make this Idyll one that will repay the most careful study. Dramatically it is an interruption of the continuity of the plot. The spasm of religious fervor has no lasting effect upon the characters, nor does it delay the inevitable retribution for the sins of the court.

FROM noiseful arms, and acts of prowess done
In tournament or tilt, Sir Percivale,
Whom Arthur and his knighthood call'd The Pure,
Had pass'd into the silent life of prayer,
Praise, fast, and alms; and leaving for the cowl   5
The helmet in an abbey far away
From Camelot, there, and not long after, died.

And one, a fellow-monk among the rest,
Ambrosius, loved him much beyond the rest,
And honor'd him, and wrought into his heart 10
A way by love that waken'd love within,
To answer that which came: and as they sat
Beneath a world-old yew-tree, darkening half
The cloisters, on a gustful April morn
That puff'd the swaying branches into smoke 15
Above them, ere the summer when he died,
The monk Ambrosius questioned Percivale:

"O brother, I have seen this yew-tree smoke,
Spring after spring, for half a hundred years.
For never have I known the world without, 20
Nor ever stray'd beyond the pale: but thee,
When first thou camest—such a courtesy
Spake thro' the limbs and in the voice—I knew
For one of those who eat in Arthur's hall;
For good ye are and bad, and like to coins, 25
Some true, some light, but every one of you
Stamp'd with the image of the King; and now
Tell me, what drove thee from the Table Round,
My brother? was it earthly passion crost?"

"Nay," said the knight; "for no such passion mine. 30
But the sweet vision of the Holy Grail
Drove me from all vainglories, rivalries,
And earthly heats that spring and sparkle out
Among us in the jousts, while women watch

Who wins, who falls; and waste the spiritual strength
Within us, better offer'd up to Heaven."   36

  To whom the monk: "The Holy Grail!—I trust
We are green in Heaven's eyes; but here too much
We moulder—as to things without I mean—
Yet one of your own knights, a guest of ours,   40
Told us of this in our refectory,
But spake with such a sadness and so low
We heard not half of what he said.   What is it?
The phantom of a cup that comes and goes?"

  "Nay, monk! what phantom?" answer'd Percivale.   45
"The cup, the cup itself, from which our Lord
Drank at the last sad supper with his own.
This, from the blessed land of Aromat—
After the day of darkness, when the dead
Went wandering o'er Moriah—the good saint,   50
Arimathean Joseph, journeying brought
To Glastonbury, where the winter thorn
Blossoms at Christmas, mindful of our Lord.
And there awhile it bode; and if a man
Could touch or see it, he was healed at once,   55
By faith, of all his ills.   But then the times
Grew to such evil that the holy cup
Was caught away to Heaven, and disappear'd."

  To whom the monk: "From our old books I know
That Joseph came of old to Glastonbury,   60
And there the heathen Prince, Arviragus,

Gave him an isle of marsh whereon to build;
And there he built with wattles from the marsh
A little lonely church in days of yore,
For so they say, these books of ours, but seem   65
Mute of this miracle, far as I have read.
But who first saw the holy thing to-day?"

"A woman," answer'd Percivale, "a nun,
And one no further off in blood from me
Than sister; and if ever holy maid   70
With knees of adoration wore the stone,
A holy maid; tho' never maiden glow'd,
But that was in her earlier maidenhood,
With such a fervent flame of human love,
Which, being rudely blunted, glanced and shot   75
Only to holy things; to prayer and praise
She gave herself, to fast and alms. And yet,
Nun as she was, the scandal of the Court,
Sin against Arthur and the Table Round,
And the strange sound of an adulterous race,   80
Across the iron grating of her cell
Beat, and she pray'd and fasted all the more.

"And he to whom she told her sins, or what
Her all but utter whiteness held for sin,
A man wellnigh a hundred winters old,   85
Spake often with her of the Holy Grail,
A legend handed down thro' five or six,
And each of these a hundred winters old,
From our Lord's time. And when King Arthur made

His Table Round, and all men's hearts became 90
Clean for a season, surely he had thought
That now the Holy Grail would come again;
But sin broke out. Ah, Christ, that it would come,
And heal the world of all their wickedness!
'O Father!' ask'd the maiden, 'might it come 95
To me by prayer and fasting?' 'Nay,' said he,
'I know not, for thy heart is pure as snow.'
And so she pray'd and fasted, till the sun
Shone, and the wind blew, thro' her, and I thought
She might have risen and floated when I saw her. 100

"For on a day she sent to speak with me.
And when she came to speak, behold her eyes
Beyond my knowing of them, beautiful,
Beyond all knowing of them, wonderful,
Beautiful in the light of holiness. 105
And 'O my brother Percivale,' she said,
'Sweet brother, I have seen the Holy Grail:
For, waked at dead of night, I heard a sound
As of a silver horn from o'er the hills
Blown, and I thought, "It is not Arthur's use 110
To hunt by moonlight;" and the slender sound
As from a distance beyond distance grew
Coming upon me—O never harp nor horn,
Nor aught we blow with breath, or touch with hand,
Was like that music as it came; and then 115
Stream'd thro' my cell a cold and silver beam,
And down the long beam stole the Holy Grail,
Rose-red with beatings in it, as if alive,

Till all the white walls of my cell were dyed
With rosy colors leaping on the wall;   120
And then the music faded, and the Grail
Past, and the beam decay'd, and from the walls
The rosy quiverings died into the night.
So now the Holy Thing is here again
Among us, brother, fast thou too and pray,   125
And tell thy brother knights to fast and pray,
That so perchance the vision may be seen
By thee and those, and all the world be heal'd.'

"Then leaving the pale nun, I spake of this
To all men; and myself fasted and pray'd   130
Always, and many among us many a week
Fasted and pray'd even to the uttermost,
Expectant of the wonder that would be.

"And one there was among us, ever moved
Among us in white armor, Galahad.   135
'God make thee good as thou art beautiful,'
Said Arthur, when he dubb'd him knight; and none
In so young youth was ever made a knight
Till Galahad: and this Galahad, when he heard
My sister's vision, fill'd me with amaze;   140
His eyes became so like her own, they seem'd
Hers, and himself her brother more than I.

"Sister or brother none had he; but some
Call'd him a son of Lancelot, and some said
Begotten by enchantment—chatterers they,   145

Like birds of passage piping up and down,
That gape for flies—we know not whence they come;
For when was Lancelot wanderingly lewd?

"But she, the wan sweet maiden, shore away
Clean from her forehead all that wealth of hair   150
Which made a silken mat-work for her feet;
And out of this she plaited broad and long
A strong sword-belt, and wove with silver thread
And crimson in the belt a strange device,
A crimson grail within a silver beam;   155
And saw the bright boy-knight, and bound it on him,
Saying, 'My knight, my love, my knight of heaven,
O thou, my love, whose love is one with mine,
I, maiden, round thee, maiden, bind my belt.
Go forth, for thou shalt see what I have seen,   160
And break thro' all, till one will crown thee king
Far in the spiritual city:' and as she spake
She sent the deathless passion in her eyes
Thro' him, and made him hers, and laid her mind
On him, and he believed in her belief.   165

"Then came a year of miracle: O brother,
In our great hall there stood a vacant chair,
Fashion'd by Merlin ere he past away,
And carven with strange figures; and in and out
The figures, like a serpent, ran a scroll   170
Of letters in a tongue no man could read.
And Merlin call'd it 'The Siege Perilous,'
Perilous for good and ill; 'for there,' he said,

'No man could sit but he should lose himself:'
And once by misadvertence Merlin sat   175
In his own chair, and so was lost; but he,
Galahad, when he heard of Merlin's doom,
Cried, 'If I lose myself, I save myself!'

"Then on a summer night it came to pass,
While the great banquet lay along the hall,   180
That Galahad would sit down in Merlin's chair.

"And all at once, as there we sat, we heard
A cracking and a riving of the roofs,
And rending, and a blast, and overhead
Thunder, and in the thunder was a cry.   185
And in the blast there smote along the hall
A beam of light seven times more clear than day:
And down the long beam stole the Holy Grail
All over cover'd with a luminous cloud,
And none might see who bare it, and it past.   190
But every knight beheld his fellow's face
As in a glory, and all the knights arose,
And staring each at other like dumb men
Stood, till I found a voice and sware a vow.

"I sware a vow before them all, that I,   195
Because I had not seen the Grail, would ride
A twelvemonth and a day in quest of it,
Until I found and saw it, as the nun
My sister saw it; and Galahad sware the vow,
And good Sir Bors, our Lancelot's cousin, sware,   200

And Lancelot sware, and many among the knights,
And Gawain sware, and louder than the rest."

Then spake the monk Ambrosius, asking him,
"What said the King?   Did Arthur take the vow?"

"Nay, for my lord," said Percivale, "the King,   205
Was not in hall: for early that same day,
Scaped thro' a cavern from a bandit hold,
An outraged maiden sprang into the hall
Crying on help: for all her shining hair
Was smear'd with earth, and either milky arm   210
Red-rent with hooks of bramble, and all she wore
Torn as a sail that leaves the rope is torn
In tempest: so the King arose and went
To smoke the scandalous hive of those wild bees
That made such honey in his realm.   Howbeit   215
Some little of this marvel he too saw,
Returning o'er the plain that then began
To darken under Camelot; whence the King
Look'd up, calling aloud, 'Lo, there! the roofs
Of our great hall are rolled in thunder-smoke!   220
Pray Heaven, they be not smitten by the bolt.'
For dear to Arthur was that hall of ours,
As having there so oft with all his knights
Feasted, and as the stateliest under heaven.

"O brother, had you known our mighty hall,   225
Which Merlin built for Arthur long ago!
For all the sacred mount of Camelot,
And all the dim rich city, roof by roof,

Tower after tower, spire beyond spire,
By grove, and garden-lawn, and rushing brook,   236
Climbs to the mighty hall that Merlin built.
And four great zones of sculpture, set betwixt
With many a mystic symbol, gird the hall:
And in the lowest beasts are slaying men,
And in the second men are slaying beasts,   235
And on the third are warriors, perfect men,
And on the fourth are men with growing wings,
And over all one statue in the mould
Of Arthur, made by Merlin, with a crown,
And peak'd wings pointed to the Northern Star.   240
And eastward fronts the statue, and the crown
And both the wings are made of gold, and flame
At sunrise till the people in far fields,
Wasted so often by the heathen hordes,
Behold it, crying, 'We have still a King.'   245

    "And, brother, had you known our hall within,
Broader and higher than any in all the lands!
Where twelve great windows blazon Arthur's wars,
And all the light that falls upon the board
Streams thro' the twelve great battles of our King. 250
Nay, one there is, and at the eastern end,
Wealthy with wandering lines of mount and mere,
Where Arthur finds the brand Excalibur.
And also one to the west, and counter to it,
And blank: and who shall blazon it? when and how?—255
O there, perchance, when all our wars are done,
The brand Excalibur will be cast away.

"So to this hall full quickly rode the King,
In horror lest the work by Merlin wrought,
Dreamlike, should on the sudden vanish, wrapt   260
In unremorseful folds of rolling fire.
And in he rode, and up I glanced, and saw
The golden dragon sparkling over all:
And many of those who burnt the hold, their arms
Hack'd, and their foreheads grimed with smoke and
     seared,   265
Follow'd, and in among bright faces, ours,
Full of the vision, prest: and then the King
Spake to me, being nearest, 'Percivale'
(Because the hall was all in tumult—some
Vowing, and some protesting), 'what is this?'   270

"O brother, when I told him what had chanced,
My sister's vision, and the rest, his face
Darken'd, as I have seen it more than once,
When some brave deed seem'd to be done in vain,
Darken; and 'Woe is me, my knights,' he cried,   275
'Had I been here, ye had not sworn the vow.'
Bold was mine answer, 'Had thyself been here,
My King, thou wouldst have sworn.'   'Yea, yea,'
     said he,
'Art thou so bold and hast not seen the Grail?'

" 'Nay, lord, I heard the sound, I saw the light,   280
But since I did not see the Holy Thing,
I sware a vow to follow it till I saw.'

"Then when he ask'd us, knight by knight, if any
Had seen it, all their answers were as one:
'Nay, lord, and therefore have we sworn our vows.' 285

" 'Lo, now,' said Arthur, 'have ye seen a cloud?
What go ye into the wilderness to see?'

"Then Galahad on the sudden, and in a voice
Shrilling along the hall to Arthur, call'd,
'But I, Sir Arthur, saw the Holy Grail, 290
I saw the Holy Grail and heard a cry—
"O Galahad, and O Galahad, follow me." '

" 'Ah, Galahad, Galahad,' said the King, 'for such
As thou art is the vision, not for these.
Thy holy nun and thou have seen a sign— 295
Holier is none, my Percivale, than she—
A sign to maim this Order which I made.
But ye, that follow but the leader's bell'
(Brother, the King was hard upon his knights)
'Taliessin is our fullest throat of song, 300
And one hath sung and all the dumb will sing.
Lancelot is Lancelot, and hath overborne
Five knights at once, and every younger knight,
Unproven, holds himself as Lancelot,
Till overborne by one, he learns—and ye, 305
What are ye? Galahads?—no, nor Percivales'
(For thus it pleased the King to range me close
After Sir Galahad); 'nay,' said he, 'but men

With strength and will to right the wrong'd, of power
To lay the sudden heads of violence flat,   310
Knights that in twelve great battles splash'd and dyed
The strong White Horse in his own heathen blood—
But one hath seen, and all the blind will see.
Go, since your vows are sacred, being made:
Yet—for ye know the cries of all my realm   315
Pass thro' this hall—how often, O my knights,
Your places being vacant at my side,
This chance of noble deeds will come and go
Unchallenged, while ye follow wandering fires
Lost in the quagmire! Many of you, yea most,   320
Return no more: ye think I show myself
Too dark a prophet: come now, let us meet
The morrow morn once more in one full field
Of gracious pastime, that once more the King,
Before ye leave him for this Quest, may count   325
The yet-unbroken strength of all his knights,
Rejoicing in that Order which he made.'

  "So when the sun broke next from under ground,
All the great table of our Arthur closed
And clash'd in such a tourney and so full,   330
So many lances broken—never yet
Had Camelot seen the like, since Arthur came:
And I myself and Galahad, for a strength
Was in us from the vision, overthrew
So many knights that all the people cried,   335
And almost burst the barriers in their heat,
Shouting, 'Sir Galahad and Sir Percivale!'

"But when the next day brake from under
    ground—
O brother, had you known our Camelot,
Built by old kings, age after age, so old   340
The King himself had fears that it would fall,
So strange, and rich, and dim; for where the roofs
Totter'd toward each other in the sky,
Met foreheads all along the street of those
Who watch'd us pass; and lower, and where the long 345
Rich galleries, lady-laden, weigh'd the necks
Of dragons clinging to the crazy walls,
Thicker than drops from thunder, showers of flowers
Fell as we past; and men and boys astride
On wyvern, lion, dragon, griffin, swan,   350
At all the corners, named us each by name,
Calling 'God speed!' but in the ways below
The knights and ladies wept, and rich and poor
Wept, and the King himself could hardly speak
For grief, and all in middle street the Queen,   355
Who rode by Lancelot, wail'd and shriek'd aloud,
'This madness has come on us for our sins.'
So to the Gate of the Three Queens we came,
Where Arthur's wars are render'd mystically,
And thence departed every one his way.   360

"And I was lifted up in heart, and thought
Of all my late-shown prowess in the lists,
How my strong lance had beaten down the knights,
So many and famous names; and never yet
Had heaven appear'd so blue, nor earth so green,   365

For all my blood danced in me, and I knew
That I should light upon the Holy Grail.

"Thereafter, the dark warning of our King,
That most of us would follow wandering fires,
Came like a driving gloom across my mind.   370
Then every evil word I had spoken once,
And every evil thought I had thought of old,
And every evil deed I ever did,
Awoke and cried, 'This Quest is not for thee.'
And lifting up mine eyes, I found myself   375
Alone, and in a land of sand and thorns,
And I was thirsty even unto death;
And I, too, cried, 'This Quest is not for thee.'

"And on I rode, and when I thought my thirst
Would slay me, saw deep lawns, and then a brook,   380
With one sharp rapid, where the crisping white
Play'd ever back upon the sloping wave,
And took both ear and eye; and o'er the brook
Were apple-trees, and apples by the brook
Fallen, and on the lawns. 'I will rest here,'   385
I said, 'I am not worthy of the Quest;'
But even while I drank the brook, and ate
The goodly apples, all these things at once
Fell into dust, and I was left alone,
And thirsting, in a land of sand and thorns.   390

"And then behold a woman at a door
Spinning; and fair the house whereby she sat,

And kind the woman's eyes and innocent,
And all her bearing gracious; and she rose
Opening her arms to meet me, as who should
    say,   395
'Rest here;' but when I touch'd her, lo! she, too,
Fell into dust and nothing, and the house
Became no better than a broken shed,
And in it a dead babe; and also this
Fell into dust, and I was left alone.   400

    "And on I rode, and greater was my thirst.
Then flash'd a yellow gleam across the world,
And where it smote the plowshare in the field,
The plowman left his plowing, and fell down
Before it; where it glitter'd on her pail,   405
The milkmaid left her milking, and fell down
Before it, and I knew not why, but thought
' The sun is rising,' tho' the sun had risen.
Then was I ware of one that on me moved
In golden armor with a crown of gold   410
About a casque all jewels; and his horse
In golden armor jewelled everywhere:
And on the splendor came, flashing me blind;
And seem'd to me the Lord of all the world,
Being so huge. But when I thought he meant   415
To crush me, moving on me, lo! he, too,
Open'd his arms to embrace me as he came,
And up I went and touch'd him, and he, too,
Fell into dust, and I was left alone
And wearying in a land of sand and thorns.   420

"And I rode on and found a mighty hill,
And on the top, a city wall'd: the spires
Prick'd with incredible pinnacles into heaven.
And by the gateway stirr'd a crowd; and these
Cried to me climbing, 'Welcome, Percivale!   425
Thou mightiest and thou purest among men!'
And glad was I and clomb, but found at top
No man, nor any voice. And thence I past
Far thro' a ruinous city, and I saw
That man had once dwelt there; but there I found 430
Only one man of an exceeding age.
'Where is that goodly company,' said I,
'That so cried out upon me?' and he had
Scarce any voice to answer, and yet gasp'd,
'Whence and what art thou?' and even as he spoke 435
Fell into dust, and disappear'd, and I
Was left alone once more, and cried in grief,
'Lo, if I find the Holy Grail itself
And touch it, it will crumble into dust.'

"And thence I dropt into a lowly vale,   440
Low as the hill was high, and where the vale
Was lowest, found a chapel, and thereby
A holy hermit in a hermitage,
To whom I told my phantoms, and he said:

"'O son, thou hast not true humility,   445
The highest virtue, mother of them all;
For when the Lord of all things made Himself
Naked of glory for His mortal change,

"Take thou my robe," she said, "for all is thine,"
And all her form shone forth with sudden light   450
So that the angels were amazed, and she
Follow'd Him down, and like a flying star
Led on the gray-hair'd wisdom of the east;
But her thou hast not known: for what is this
Thou thoughtest of thy prowess and thy sins?   455
Thou hast not lost thyself to save thyself
As Galahad.' When the hermit made an end,
In silver armor suddenly Galahad shone
Before us, and against the chapel door
Laid lance, and enter'd, and we knelt in prayer.   460
And there the hermit slaked my burning thirst,
And at the sacring of the mass I saw
The holy elements alone; but he,
'Saw ye no more? I, Galahad, saw the Grail,
The Holy Grail, descend upon the shrine: 465
I saw the fiery face as of a child
That smote itself into the bread, and went;
And hither am I come; and never yet
Hath what thy sister taught me first to see,
This Holy Thing, fail'd from my side, nor come   470
Covered, but moving with me night and day,
Fainter by day, but always in the night
Blood-red, and sliding down the blacken'd marsh
Blood-red, and on the naked mountain-top
Blood-red, and in the sleeping mere below   475
Blood-red. And in the strength of this I rode,
Shattering all evil customs everywhere,
And past thro' Pagan realms, and made them mine,

And clash'd with Pagan hordes, and bore them down
And broke thro' all, and in the strength of this   480
Come victor. But my time is hard at hand,
And hence I go; and one will crown me king
Far in the spiritual city; and come thou, too,
For thou shalt see the vision when I go.'

"While thus he spake, his eye, dwelling on mine   485
Drew me, with power upon me, till I grew
One with him, to believe as he believed.
Then, when the day began to wane, we went.

"There rose a hill that none but man could climb,
Scarr'd with a hundred wintry watercourses—   490
Storm at the top, and when we gained it, storm
Round us and death; for every moment glanced
His silver arms and gloom'd: so quick and thick
The lightnings here and there to left and right
Struck, till the dry old trunks about us, dead,   495
Yea, rotten with a hundred years of death,
Sprang into fire: and at the base we found
On either hand, as far as eye could see,
A great black swamp and of an evil smell,
Part black, part whiten'd with the bones of men,   500
Not to be crost, save that some ancient king
Had built a way, where, link'd with many a bridge,
A thousand piers ran into the great Sea.
And Galahad fled along them bridge by bridge,
And every bridge as quickly as he crost   505

Sprang into fire and vanish'd, though I yearn'd
To follow; and thrice above him all the heavens
Open'd and blazed with thunder such as seem'd
Shoutings of all the sons of God: and first
At once I saw him far on the great Sea, 510
In silver-shining armor starry-clear;
And o'er his head the Holy Vessel hung
Clothed in white samite or a luminous cloud.
And with exceeding swiftness ran the boat,
If boat it were—I saw not whence it came. 515
And when the heavens open'd and blazed again
Roaring, I saw him like a silver star—
And had he set the sail, or had the boat
Become a living creature clad with wings?
And o'er his head the Holy Vessel hung 520
Redder than any rose, a joy to me,
For now I knew the veil had been withdrawn.
Then in a moment when they blazed again
Opening, I saw the least of little stars
Down on the waste, and straight beyond the star 525
I saw the spiritual city and all her spires
And gateways in a glory like one pearl—
No larger, tho' the goal of all the saints—
Strike from the sea; and from the star there shot
A rose-red sparkle to the city, and there 530
Dwelt, and I knew it was the Holy Grail,
Which never eyes on earth again shall see.
Then fell the floods of heaven drowning the deep.
And how my feet recrost the deathful ridge
No memory in me lives; but that I touch'd 535

The chapel-doors at dawn I know; and thence
Taking my war-horse from the holy man,
Glad that no phantom vext me more, return'd
To whence I came, the gate of Arthur's wars."

"O brother," ask'd Ambrosius,—"for in sooth   540
These ancient books—and they would win thee—
   teem,
Only I find not there this Holy Grail,
With miracles and marvels like to these,
Not all unlike; which oftentime I read,
Who read but on my breviary with ease,   545
Till my head swims; and then go forth and pass
Down to the little thorpe that lies so close,
And almost plaster'd like a martin's nest
To these old walls—and mingle with our folk;
And knowing every honest face of theirs   550
As well as ever shepherd knew his sheep,
And every homely secret in their hearts,
Delight myself with gossip and old wives,
And ills and aches, and teethings, lyings-in,
And mirthful sayings, children of the place,   555
That have no meaning half a league away:
Or lulling random squabbles when they rise,
Chafferings and chatterings at the market-cross,
Rejoice, small man, in this small world of mine,
Yea, even in their hens and in their eggs—   560
O brother, saving this Sir Galahad,
Came ye on none but phantoms in your quest,
No man, no woman?"

Then Sir Percivale:
"All men, to one so bound by such a vow,
And women were as phantoms. O, my brother,   565
Why wilt thou shame me to confess to thee
How far I falter'd from my quest and vow?
For after I had lain so many nights,
A bedmate of the snail and eft and snake,
In grass and burdock, I was changed to wan   570
And meagre, and the vision had not come;
And then I chanced upon a goodly town
With one great dwelling in the middle of it;
Thither I made, and there was I disarm'd
By maidens each as fair as any flower: 575
But when they led me into hall, behold,
The Princess of that castle was the one,
Brother, and that one only, who had ever
Made my heart leap; for when I moved of old
A slender page about her father's hall,   580
And she a slender maiden, all my heart
Went after her with longing: yet we twain
Had never kiss'd a kiss, or vow'd a vow.
And now I came upon her once again,
And one had wedded her, and he was dead,   585
And all his land and wealth and state were hers.
And while I tarried, every day she set
A banquet richer than the day before
By me; for all her longing and her will
Was toward me as of old; till one fair morn,   590
I walking to and fro beside a stream
That flash'd across her orchard underneath

Her castle-walls, she stole upon my walk,
And calling me the greatest of all knights,
Embraced me, and so kiss'd me the first time,　　595
And gave herself and all her wealth to me.
Then I remember'd Arthur's warning word,
That most of us would follow wandering fires,
And the Quest faded in my heart.　Anon,
The heads of all her people drew to me,　　600
With supplication both of knees and tongue:
'We have heard of thee: thou art our greatest knight,
Our Lady says it, and we well believe:
Wed thou our Lady, and rule over us,
And thou shalt be as Arthur in our land.'　　605
O me, my brother! but one night my vow
Burnt me within, so that I rose and fled,
But wail'd and wept, and hated mine own self,
And even the Holy Quest, and all but her;
Then after I was join'd with Galahad　　610
Cared not for her, nor anything upon earth."

Then said the monk, "Poor men, when yule is
　　cold,
Must be content to sit by little fires.
And this am I, so that ye care for me
Ever so little; yea, and blest be Heaven　　615
That brought thee here to this poor house of ours
Where all the brethren are so hard, to warm
My cold heart with a friend: but O the pity
To find thine own first love once more—to hold,
Hold her a wealthy bride within thine arms,　　620

Or all but hold, and then—cast her aside,
Foregoing all her sweetness, like a weed.
For we that want the warmth of double life,
We that are plagued with dreams of something sweet
Beyond all sweetness in a life so rich,—   625
Ah, blessed Lord, I speak too earthly-wise,
Seeing I never stray'd beyond the cell,
But live like an old badger in his earth,
With earth about him everywhere, despite
All fast and penance.   Saw ye none beside,   630
None of your knights?"

               "Yea so," said Percivale:
"One night my pathway swerving east, I saw
The pelican on the casque of our Sir Bors
All in the middle of the rising moon:
And toward him spurr'd, and hail'd him, and he me,
And each made joy of either; then he ask'd,   635
'Where is he? hast thou seen him—Lancelot?—Once,'
Said good Sir Bors, 'he dash'd across me—mad,
And maddening what he rode: and when I cried,
"Ridest thou then so hotly on a quest   640
So holy?" Lancelot shouted, "Stay me not!
I have been the sluggard, and I ride apace,
For now there is a lion in the way."
So vanish'd.'

            "Then Sir Bors had ridden on
Softly, and sorrowing for our Lancelot,   645
Because his former madness, once the talk

And scandal of our table, had return'd;
For Lancelot's kith and kin so worship him
That ill to him is ill to them; to Bors
Beyond the rest; he well had been content   650
Not to have seen, so Lancelot might have seen,
The Holy Cup of healing; and, indeed,
Being so clouded with his grief and love,
Small heart was his after the Holy Quest:
If God would send the vision, well; if not,   655
The Quest and he were in the hands of Heaven.

    "And then, with small adventure met, Sir Bors
Rode to the lonest tract of all the realm,
And found a people there among their crags,
Our race and blood, a remnant that were left   660
Paynim amid their circles, and the stones
They pitch up straight to heaven: and their wise men
Were strong in that old magic which can trace
The wandering of the stars, and scoff'd at him
And this high Quest as at a simple thing: 665
Told him he follow'd—almost Arthur's words—
A mocking fire: 'what other fire than he,
Whereby the blood beats and the blossom blows,
And the sea rolls, and all the world is warm'd?'
And when his answer chafed them, the rough crowd,
Hearing he had a difference with their priests,   671
Seized him, and bound and plunged him into a cell
Of great piled stones; and lying bounden there
In darkness thro' innumerable hours
He heard the hollow-ringing heavens sweep   675

Over him, till by miracle—what else?—
Heavy as it was, a great stone slipt and fell,
Such as no wind could move: and thro' the gap
Glimmer'd the streaming scud: then came a night
Still as the day was loud; and through the gap   680
The seven clear stars of Arthur's Table Round—
For, brother, so one night, because they roll
Thro' such a round in heaven, we named the stars,
Rejoicing in ourselves and in our King—
And these, like bright eyes of familiar friends,   685
In on him shone: 'And then to me, to me,'
Said good Sir Bors, 'beyond all hopes of mine,
Who scarce had pray'd or ask'd it for myself—
Across the seven clear stars—O grace to me—
In color like the fingers of a hand   690
Before a burning taper, the sweet Grail
Glided and past, and close upon it peal'd
A sharp quick thunder.'   Afterwards, a maid,
Who kept our holy faith among her kin
In secret, entering, loosed and let him go."   695

To whom the monk: "And I remember now
That pelican on the casque: Sir Bors it was
Who spake so low and sadly at our board;
And mighty reverent at our grace was he:
A square-set man and honest; and his eyes,   700
An out-door sign of all the warmth within,
Smiled with his lips—a smile beneath a cloud,
But heaven had meant it for a sunny one:
Ay, ay, Sir Bors, who else? But when ye reach'd

The city, found ye all your knights return'd,   705
Or was there sooth in Arthur's prophecy,
Tell me, and what said each, and what the King?"

Then answer'd Percivale: "And that can I,
Brother, and truly; since the living words
Of so great men as Lancelot and our King   710
Pass not from door to door and out again,
But sit within the house.   O, when we reach'd
The city, our horses stumbling as they trode
On heaps of ruin, hornless unicorns,
Crack'd basilisks, and splinter'd cockatrices,   715
And shatter'd talbots, which had left the stones
Raw, that they fell from, brought us to the hall.

"And there sat Arthur on the daïs-throne,
And those that had gone out upon the Quest
Wasted and worn, and but a tithe of them,   720
And those that had not, stood before the King,
Who, when he saw me, rose and bade me hail,
Saying, 'A welfare in thine eye reproves
Our fear of some disastrous chance for thee
On hill, or plain, at sea, or flooding ford.   725
So fierce a gale made havoc here of late
Among the strange devices of our kings;
Yea, shook this newer, stronger hall of ours,
And from the statue Merlin moulded for us
Half-wrench'd a golden wing; but now—the Quest,
This vision—hast thou seen the Holy Cup,   731
That Joseph brought of old to Glastonbury?'

"So when I told him all thyself hast heard,
Ambrosius, and my fresh but fixt resolve
To pass away into the quiet life,   735
He answer'd not, but, sharply turning, ask'd
Of Gawain, 'Gawain, was this Quest for thee?'

" 'Nay, lord,' said Gawain, 'not for such as I.
Therefore I communed with a saintly man,
Who made me sure the Quest was not for me;   740
For I was much awearied of the Quest:
But found a silk pavilion in a field,
And merry maidens in it; and then this gale
Tore my pavilion from the tenting-pin,
And blew my merry maidens all about   745
With all discomfort; yea, and but for this,
My twelvemonth and a day were pleasant to me.'

"He ceased; and Arthur turn'd to whom at first
He saw not, for Sir Bors, on entering, push'd
Athwart the throng to Lancelot, caught his hand,   750
Held it, and there, half-hidden by him, stood,
Until the King espied him, saying to him,
'Hail, Bors! If ever loyal man and true
Could see it, thou hast seen the Grail;' and Bors,
'Ask me not, for I may not speak of it: 755
I saw it:' and the tears were in his eyes.

"Then there remain'd but Lancelot, for the rest
Spake but of sundry perils in the storm;
Perhaps, like him of Cana in Holy Writ,

Our Arthur kept his best until the last;   760
'Thou, too, my Lancelot,' ask'd the King, 'my friend,
Our mightiest, hath this Quest avail'd for thee?'

    " 'Our mightiest!' answer'd Lancelot, with a groan;
'O King!'—and when he paused, methought I spied
A dying fire of madness in his eyes—   765
'O King, my friend, if friend of thine I be,
Happier are those that welter in their sin,
Swine in the mud, that cannot see for slime,
Slime of the ditch: but in me lived a sin
So strange, of such a kind, that all of pure,   770
Noble, and knightly in me twined and clung
Round that one sin, until the wholesome flower
And poisonous grew together, each as each,
Not to be pluck'd asunder; and when thy knights
Sware, I sware with them only in the hope   775
That could I touch or see the Holy Grail
They might be pluck'd asunder. Then I spake
To one most holy saint, who wept and said
That, save they could be pluck'd asunder, all
My quest were but in vain; to whom I vow'd   780
That I would work according as he will'd.
And forth I went, and while I yearn'd and strove
To tear the twain asunder in my heart,
My madness came upon me as of old,
And whipt me into waste fields far away;   785
There was I beaten down by little men,
Mean knights, to whom the moving of my sword
And shadow of my spear had been enow

To scare them from me once; and then I came
All in my folly to the naked shore, 790
Wide flats, where nothing but coarse grasses grew;
But such a blast, my King, began to blow,
So loud a blast along the shore and sea,
Ye could not hear the waters for the blast,
Tho' heapt in mounds and ridges all the sea 795
Drove like a cataract, and all the sand
Swept like a river, and the clouded heavens
Were shaken with the motion and the sound.
And blackening on the sea-foam swayed a boat,
Half-swallow'd in it, anchor'd with a chain; 800
And in my madness to myself I said,
'I will embark and I will lose myself,
And in the great sea wash away my sin."
I burst the chain, I sprang into the boat.
Seven days I drove along the dreary deep, 805
And with me drove the moon and all the stars;
And the wind fell, and on the seventh night
I heard the shingle grinding in the surge,
And felt the boat shock earth, and looking up,
Behold, the enchanted towers of Carbonek, 810
A castle like a rock upon a rock,
With chasm-like portals open to the sea,
And steps that met the breaker! there was none
Stood near it but a lion on each side
That kept the entry, and the moon was full. 815
Then from the boat I leapt, and up the stairs.
There drew my sword. With sudden-flaring manes
Those two great beasts rose upright like a man,

Each gript a shoulder, and I stood between;
And, when I would have smitten them, heard a
    voice, 820
"Doubt not, go forward; if thou doubt, the beasts
Will tear thee piecemeal." Then with violence
The sword was dash'd from out my hand, and fell.
And up into the sounding hall I past;
But nothing in the sounding hall I saw, 825
No bench nor table, painting on the wall
Or shield of knight; only the rounded moon
Thro' the tall oriel on the rolling sea.
But always in the quiet house I heard,
Clear as a lark, high o'er me as a lark, 830
A sweet voice singing in the topmost tower
To the eastward: up I climb'd a thousand steps
With pain: as in a dream I seem'd to climb
For ever: at the last I reach'd a door,
A light was in the crannies, and I heard, 835
"Glory and joy and honor to our Lord
And to the Holy Vessel of the Grail."
Then in my madness I essay'd the door;
It gave; and thro' a stormy glare, a heat
As from a seven-times-heated furnace, I, 840
Blasted and burnt, and blinded as I was,
With such a fierceness that I swoon'd away—
O, yet methought I saw the Holy Grail,
All pall'd in crimson samite, and around
Great angels, awful shapes, and wings and eyes. 845
And but for all my madness and my sin,
And then my swooning, I had sworn I saw

That which I saw; but what I saw was veil'd
And cover'd; and this Quest was not for me.'

  "So speaking, and here ceasing, Lancelot left   850
The hall long silent, till Sir Gawain—nay,
Brother, I need not tell thee foolish words,—
A reckless and irreverent knight was he,
Now bolden'd by the silence of his King,—
Well, I will tell thee: 'O King, my liege,' he said,
'Hath Gawain fail'd in any quest of thine?   856
When have I stinted stroke in foughten field?
But as for thine, my good friend Percivale,
Thy holy nun and thou have driven men mad,
Yea, made our mightiest madder than our least.   860
But by mine eyes and by mine ears I swear,
I will be deafer than the blue-eyed cat,
And thrice as blind as any noonday owl,
To holy virgins in their ecstasies,
Henceforward.'

              " 'Deafer,' said the blameless King,
'Gawain, and blinder unto holy things   866
Hope not to make thyself by idle vows,
Being too blind to have desire to see.
But if indeed there came a sign from heaven,
Blessed are Bors, Lancelot, and Percivale,   870
For these have seen according to their sight.
For every fiery prophet in old times,
And all the sacred madness of the bard,
When God made music thro' them, could but speak

His music by the framework and the chord;   87?
And as ye saw it ye have spoken truth.

" 'Nay—but thou errest, Lancelot: never yet
Could all of true and noble in knight and man
Twine round one sin, whatever it might be,
With such a closeness but apart there grew,   880
Save that he were the swine thou spakest of,
Some root of knighthood and pure nobleness;
Whereto see thou, that it may bear its flower.

" 'And spake I not too truly, O my knights?
Was I too dark a prophet when I said   88?
To those who went upon the Holy Quest,
That most of them would follow wandering fires,
Lost in the quagmire?—lost to me and gone,
And left me gazing at a barren board,
And a lean Order—scarce return'd a tithe—   890
And out of those to whom the vision came
My greatest hardly will believe he saw;
Another hath beheld it afar off,
And leaving human wrongs to right themselves,
Cares but to pass into the silent life.   89?
And one hath had the vision face to face,
And now his chair desires him here in vain,
However they may crown him otherwhere.

" 'And some among you held, that if the King
Had seen the sight he would have sworn the vow;   90?
Not easily, seeing that the King must guard

That which he rules, and is but as the hind
To whom a space of land is given to plow.
Who may not wander from the alloted field
Before his work be done; but, being done,　　905
Let visions of the night or of the day
Come, as they will; and many a time they come
Until this earth he walks on seems not earth,
This light that strikes his eyeball is not light,
This air that smites his forehead is not air　　910
But vision—yea, his very hand and foot—
In moments when he feels he cannot die,
And knows himself no vision to himself,
Nor the high God a vision, nor that One
Who rose again: ye have seen what ye have seen.'

"So spake the King: I knew not all he meant."　　91₉

GUINEVERE

The ranks of Arthur's Knights, decimated by the quest of the Holy Grail, are filled by new men, among them Pelleas, the Gareth of the later Idylls. But no longer does a healthful people live in Arthur's realm. "Pelleas and Ettarre" and "The Last Tournament," following "The Holy Grail," are revolting stories, needful to be told, perhaps, to show the degradation of the realm.

"Guinevere" begins with the King's discovery of his wife's sin. The scenes are conceived with remarkable dramatic power and are portrayed in the finest poetry in the whole cycle of the Idylls. Here culminates the Queen's struggle with her conscience wherein she breaks the bonds that Lancelot's madness could not sever. Throughout the poem Tennyson reaches down into the fundamentals of life and character:—

> But help me, Heaven, for surely I repent!
> For what is true repentance but in thought—
> Not even in inmost thought to think again
> The sins that made the past so pleasant to us?
> And I have sworn never to see him more,
> To see him more.

QUEEN GUINEVERE had fled the court, and sat
There in the holy house at Almesbury
Weeping, none with her save a little maid,
A novice: one low light betwixt them burn'd
Blurr'd by the creeping mist, for all abroad,   5
Beneath a moon unseen albeit at full,
The white mist, like a face-cloth to the face,
Clung to the dead earth, and the land was still.

For hither had she fled, her cause of flight
Sir Modred; he that like a subtle beast   10
Lay couchant with his eyes upon the throne,
Ready to spring, waiting a chance: for this
He chill'd the popular praises of the King
With silent smiles of slow disparagement;
And tamper'd with the Lords of the White Horse,   15
Heathen, the brood by Hengist left; and sought
To make disruption in the Table Round
Of Arthur, and to splinter it into feuds
Serving his traitorous end; and all his aims
Were sharpen'd by strong hate for Lancelot.   20

For thus it chanced one morn when all the court,
Green-suited, but with plumes that mock'd the may,
Had been—their wont—a-maying and return'd,
That Modred still in green, all ear and eye,
Climb'd to the high top of the garden-wall   25
To spy some secret scandal if he might,
And saw the Queen who sat betwixt her best
Enid and lissome Vivien, of her court
The wiliest and the worst; and more than this
He saw not, for Sir Lancelot passing by   30
Spied where he couch'd, and as the gardener's hand
Picks from the colewort a green caterpillar,
So from the high wall and the flowering grove
Of grasses Lancelot pluck'd him by the heel,
And cast him as a worm upon the way;   35
But when he knew the prince tho' marr'd with dust,
He, reverencing king's blood in a bad man,

Made such excuses as he might, and these
Full knightly without scorn: for in those days
No knight of Arthur's noblest dealt in scorn;   40
But, if a man were halt, or hunch'd, in him
By those whom God had made full-limb'd and tall,
Scorn was allow'd as part of his defect,
And he was answer'd softly by the King
And all his Table. So Sir Lancelot holp   45
To raise the prince, who rising twice or thrice
Full sharply smote his knees, and smiled, and went:
But, ever after, the small violence done
Rankled in him and ruffled all his heart,
As the sharp wind that ruffles all day long   50
A little bitter pool about a stone
On the bare coast.

                        But when Sir Lancelot told
This matter to the Queen, at first she laugh'd
Lightly, to think of Modred's dusty fall,
Then shudder'd, as the village wife who cries,   55
"I shudder, some one steps across my grave;"
Then laugh'd again, but faintlier, for indeed
She half-foresaw that he, the subtle beast,
Would track her guilt until he found, and hers
Would be for evermore a name of scorn.   60
Henceforward rarely could she front in hall,
Or elsewhere, Modred's narrow foxy face,
Heart-hiding smile, and gray persistent eye.
Henceforward too, the Powers that tend the soul,
To help it from the death that cannot die,   65

And save it even in extremes, began
To vex and plague her.   Many a time for hours,
Beside the placid breathings of the King,
In the dead night, grim faces came and went
Before her, or a vague spiritual fear—   70
Like to some doubtful noise of creaking doors,
Heard by the watcher in a haunted house,
That keeps the rust of murder on the walls—
Held her awake: or if she slept she dream'd
An awful dream; for then she seem'd to stand   75
On some vast plain before a setting sun,
And from the sun there swiftly made at her
A ghastly something, and its shadow flew
Before it till it touch'd her, and she turn'd—
When lo! her own, that broadening from her feet,   80
And blackening, swallow'd all the land, and in it
Far cities burnt, and with a cry she woke.
And all this trouble did not pass but grew,
Till even the clear face of the guileless King,
And trustful courtesies of household life,   85
Became her bane; and at the last she said,
"O Lancelot, get thee hence to thine own land,
For if thou tarry we shall meet again,
And if we meet again some evil chance
Will make the smouldering scandal break and blaze   90
Before the people and our lord the King."
And Lancelot ever promised, but remain'd,
And still they met and met.   Again she said,
"O Lancelot, if thou love me get thee hence."
And then they were agreed upon a night—   95

When the good King should not be there—to meet
And part for ever. Vivien, lurking, heard.
She told Sir Modred. Passion-pale they met
And greeted. Hands in hands, and eye to eye,
Low on the border of her couch they sat	100
Stammering and staring. It was their last hour,
A madness of farewells. And Modred brought
His creatures to the basement of the tower
For testimony; and crying with full voice,
"Traitor, come out, ye are trapt at last," aroused	105
Lancelot, who rushing outward lionlike
Leapt on him, and hurl'd him headlong, and he fell
Stunn'd, and his creatures took and bare him off,
And all was still. Then she, "The end is come,
And I am shamed for ever"; and he said:	110
"Mine be the shame; mine was the sin: but rise,
And fly to my strong castle over-seas:
There will I hide thee till my life shall end,
There hold thee with my life against the world."
She answer'd: "Lancelot, wilt thou hold me so?	115
Nay, friend, for we have taken our farewells.
Would God that thou couldst hide me from myself!
Mine is the shame, for I was wife, and thou
Unwedded; yet rise now, and let us fly,
For I will draw me into sanctuary,	120
And bide my doom." So Lancelot got her horse,
Set her thereon, and mounted on his own,
And then they rode to the divided way,
There kiss'd, and parted weeping: for he past,
Love-loyal to the least wish of the Queen,	125

Back to his land; but she to Almesbury
Fled all night long by glimmering waste and weald,
And heard the spirits of the waste and weald
Moan as she fled, or thought she heard them moan:
And in herself she moan'd, "Too late, too late!"   130
Till in the cold wind that foreruns the morn,
A blot in heaven, the raven, flying high,
Croak'd, and she thought, "He spies a field of death;
For now the heathen of the Northern Sea,
Lured by the crimes and frailties of the court,   135
Begin to slay the folk and spoil the land."

   And when she came to Almesbury she spake
There to the nuns, and said, "Mine enemies
Pursue me, but, O peaceful Sisterhood,
Receive and yield me sanctuary, nor ask   140
Her name to whom ye yield it till her time
To tell you"; and her beauty, grace, and power
Wrought as a charm upon them, and they spared
To ask it.

            So the stately Queen abode
For many a week, unknown, among the nuns,   145
Nor with them mix'd, nor told her name, nor sought,
Wrapt in her grief, for housel or for shrift,
But communed only with the little maid,
Who pleased her with a babbling heedlessness
Which often lured her from herself; but now,   150
This night, a rumor wildly blown about
Came that Sir Modred had usurp'd the realm

And leagued him with the heathen, while the King
Was waging war on Lancelot: then she thought,
"With what a hate the people and the King   155
Must hate me," and bow'd down upon her hands
Silent, until the little maid, who brook'd
No silence, brake it, uttering "Late! so late!
What hour, I wonder now?" and when she drew
No answer, by and by began to hum   160
An air the nuns had taught her: "Late, so late!"
Which when she heard, the Queen look'd up, and
            said,
"O maiden, if indeed ye list to sing,
Sing, and unbind my heart that I may weep."
Whereat full willingly sang the little maid.   165

    "Late, late, so late! and dark the night and chill!
Late, late, so late! but we can enter still.
Too late, too late! ye cannot enter now.

    "No light had we: for that we do repent,
And learning this, the bridegroom will relent.   170
Too late, too late! ye cannot enter now.

    "No light: so late! and dark and chill the night!
O, let us in, that we may find the light!
Too late, too late, ye cannot enter now!

    "Have we not heard the bridegroom is so sweet? 175
O, let us in, tho' late, to kiss his feet!
No, no, too late! ye cannot enter now."

So sang the novice, while full passionately,
Her head upon her hands, remembering
Her thought when first she came, wept the sad Queen.
Then said the little novice prattling to her: 181

"O pray you, noble lady, weep no more;
But let my words—the words of one so small,
Who knowing nothing knows but to obey,
And if I do not there is penance given—   185
Comfort your sorrows; for they do not flow
From evil done: right sure am I of that,
Who see your tender grace and stateliness.
But weigh your sorrows with our lord the King's,
And weighing find them less; for gone is he   190
To wage grim war against Sir Lancelot there,
Round that strong castle where he holds the Queen;
And Modred whom he left in charge of all,
The traitor—Ah, sweet lady, the King's grief
For his own self, and his own Queen, and realm,   195
Must needs be thrice as great as any of ours!
For me, I thank the saints, I am not great;
For if there ever come a grief to me
I cry my cry in silence, and have done:
None knows it, and my tears have brought me good.
But even were the griefs of little ones   201
As great as those of great ones, yet this grief
Is added to the griefs the great must bear,
That, howsoever much they may desire
Silence, they cannot weep behind a cloud;   205
As even here they talk at Almesbury

About the good King and his wicked Queen,
And were I such a King with such a Queen,
Well might I wish to veil her wickedness,
But were I such a King it could not be."   210

Then to her own sad heart mutter'd the Queen,
"Will the child kill me with her innocent talk?"
But openly she answer'd, "Must not I,
If this false traitor have displaced his lord,
Grieve with the common grief of all the realm?"   215

"Yea," said the maid, "this is all woman's grief,
That *she* is woman, whose disloyal life
Hath wrought confusion in the Table Round
Which good King Arthur founded, years ago,
With signs and miracles and wonders, there   220
At Camelot, ere the coming of the Queen."

Then thought the Queen within herself again,
"Will the child kill me with her foolish prate?"
But openly she spake and said to her,
"O little maid, shut in by nunnery walls,   225
What canst thou know of Kings and Tables Round,
Or what of signs and wonders, but the signs
And simple miracles of thy nunnery?"

To whom the little novice garrulously:
"Yea, but I know: the land was full of signs   230
And wonders ere the coming of the Queen.
So said my father, and himself was knight

Of the great Table—at the founding of it,
And rode thereto from Lyonnesse; and he said
That as he rode, an hour or maybe twain   235
After the sunset, down the coast, he heard
Strange music, and he paused, and turning—there,
All down the lonely coast of Lyonnesse,
Each with a beacon-star upon his head,
And with a wild sea-light about his feet,   240
He saw them—headland after headland flame
Far on into the rich heart of the west:
And in the light the white mermaiden swam,
And strong man-breasted things stood from the sea,
And sent a deep sea-voice thro' all the land,   245
To which the little elves of chasm and cleft
Made answer, sounding like a distant horn.
So said my father—yea, and furthermore,
Next morning, while he past the dim-lit woods,
Himself beheld three spirits mad with joy   250
Come dashing down on a tall wayside flower,
That shook beneath them as the thistle shakes
When three gray linnets wrangle for the seed:
And still at evenings on before his horse
The flickering fairy-circle wheel'd and broke   255
Flying, and link'd again, and wheel'd and broke
Flying, for all the land was full of life.
And when at last he came to Camelot,
A wreath of airy dancers hand-in-hand
Swung round the lighted lantern of the hall;   260
And in the hall itself was such a feast
As never man had dream'd; for every knight

Had whatsoever meat he long'd for served
By hands unseen; and even as he said
Down in the cellars merry bloated things   265
Shoulder'd the spigot, straddling on the butts
While the wine ran: so glad were spirits and men
Before the coming of the sinful Queen."

Then spake the Queen and somewhat bitterly,
"Were they so glad? ill prophets were they all,   270
Spirits and men: could none of them foresee,
Not even thy wise father with his signs
And wonders, what has fallen upon the realm?"

To whom the novice garrulously again:
"Yea, one, a bard; of whom my father said,   275
Full many a noble war-song had he sung,
Even in the presence of an enemy's fleet,
Between the steep cliff and the coming wave;
And many a mystic lay of life and death
Had chanted on the smoky mountain-tops,   280
When round him bent the spirits of the hills
With all their dewy hair blown back like flame.
So said my father—and that night the bard
Sang Arthur's glorious wars, and sang the King
As wellnigh more than man, and rail'd at those   285
Who call'd him the false son of Gorloïs:
For there was no man knew from whence he came;
But after tempest, when the long wave broke
All down the thundering shores of Bude and Bos,
There came a day as still as heaven, and then   290

They found a naked child upon the sands
Of dark Tintagil by the Cornish sea,
And that was Arthur; and they foster'd him
Till he by miracle was approven King:
And that his grave should be a mystery   295
From all men, like his birth; and could he find
A woman in her womanhood as great
As he was in his manhood, then, he sang,
The twain together well might change the world.
But even in the middle of his song   300
He falter'd, and his hand fell from the harp,
And pale he turn'd, and reel'd, and would have
          fallen,
But that they stay'd him up; nor would he tell
His vision; but what doubt that he foresaw
This evil work of Lancelot and the Queen?"   305

Then thought the Queen, "Lo! they have set her
          on,
Our simple-seeming abbess and her nuns,
To play upon me," and bow'd her head nor spake.
Whereat the novice crying, with clasp'd hands,
Shame on her own garrulity garrulously,   310
Said the good nuns would check her gadding tongue
Full often, "and, sweet lady, if I seem
To vex an ear too sad to listen to me,
Unmannerly, with prattling and the tales
Which my good father told me, check me too   315
Nor let me shame my father's memory, one
Of noblest manners, tho' himself would say

Sir Lancelot had the noblest; and he died,
Kill'd in a tilt, come next, five summers back,
And left me; but of others who remain,   320
And of the two first-famed for courtesy—
And pray you check me if I ask amiss—
But pray you, which had noblest, while you moved
Among them, Lancelot or our lord the King?"

Then the pale Queen look'd up and answer'd
        her:
"Sir Lancelot, as became a noble knight,   325
Was gracious to all ladies, and the same
In open battle or the tilting-field
Forbore his own advantage, and the King
In open battle or the tilting-field   330
Forbore his own advantage, and these two
Were the most nobly-manner'd men of all;
For manners are not idle, but the fruit
Of loyal nature and of noble mind."

"Yea," said the maid, "be manners such fair
        fruit?
Then Lancelot's needs must be a thousand-fold   335
Less noble, being, as all rumor runs,
The most disloyal friend in all the world."

To which a mournful answer made the Queen:
"O, closed about by narrowing nunnery-walls,   340
What knowest thou of the world and all its lights
And shadows, all the wealth and all the woe?

If ever Lancelot, that most noble knight,
Were for one hour less noble than himself,
Pray for him that he scape the doom of fire,   345
And weep for her who drew him to his doom."

"Yea," said the little novice, "I pray for both;
But I should all as soon believe that his,
Sir Lancelot's, were as noble as the King's,
As I could think, sweet lady, yours would be   350
Such as they are, were you the sinful Queen."

So she, like many another babbler, hurt
Whom she would soothe, and harm'd where she would
          heal;
For here a sudden flush of wrathful heat
Fired all the pale face of the Queen, who cried: 355
"Such as thou art be never maiden more
For ever! thou their tool, set on to plague
And play upon and harry me, petty spy
And traitress!"   When that storm of anger brake
From Guinevere, aghast the maiden rose,   360
White as her veil, and stood before the Queen
As tremulously as foam upon the beach
Stands in a wind, ready to break and fly,
And when the Queen had added, "Get thee hence!"
Fled frighted.   Then that other left alone   365
Sigh'd, and began to gather heart again,
Saying in herself: "The simple, fearful child
Meant nothing, but my own too-fearful guilt,
Simpler than any child, betrays itself.

But help me, Heaven, for surely I repent!   370
For what is true repentance but in thought—
Not even in inmost thought to think again
The sins that made the past so pleasant to us?
And I have sworn never to see him more,
To see him more."

                And even in saying this,   375
Her memory from old habit of the mind
Went slipping back upon the golden days
In which she saw him first, when Lancelot came,
Reputed the best knight and goodliest man,
Ambassador, to yield her to his lord   380
Arthur, and led her forth, and far ahead
Of his and her retinue moving, they,
Rapt in sweet talk or lively, all on love
And sport and tilts and pleasure,—for the time
Was may-time, and as yet no sin was dream'd,—   385
Rode under groves that look'd a paradise
Of blossom, over sheets of hyacinth
That seem'd the heavens upbreaking thro' the earth,
And on from hill to hill, and every day
Beheld at noon in some delicious dale   390
The silk pavilions of King Arthur raised
For brief repast or afternoon repose
By couriers gone before; and on again,
Till yet once more ere set of sun they saw
The Dragon of the great Pendragonship,   395
That crown'd the state pavilion of the King,
Blaze by the rushing brook or silent well.

But when the Queen immersed in such a trance,
And moving thro' the past unconsciously,
Came to that point where first she saw the King   400
Ride toward her from the city, sigh'd to find
Her journey done, glanced at him, thought him cold,
High, self-contain'd, and passionless, not like him,
"Not like my Lancelot"—while she brooded thus
And grew half-guilty in her thoughts again,   405
There rode an armed warrior to the doors.
A murmuring whisper thro' the nunnery ran,
Then on a sudden a cry, "The King!" She sat
Stift-stricken, listening; but when armed feet
Thro' the long gallery from the outer doors   410
Rang coming, prone from off her seat she fell,
And grovell'd with her face against the floor.
There with her milk-white arms and shadowy hair
She made her face a darkness from the King,
And in the darkness heard his armed feet   415
Pause by her; then came silence, then a voice,
Monotonous and hollow like a ghost's
Denouncing judgment, but, tho' changed, the King's:

"Liest thou here so low, the child of one
I honor'd, happy, dead before thy shame?   420
Well is it that no child is born of thee.
The children born of thee are sword and fire,
Red ruin, and the breaking up of laws,
The craft of kindred and the godless hosts
Of heathen swarming o'er the Northern Sea;   425
Whom I, while yet Sir Lancelot, my right arm,

The mightiest of my knights, abode with me,
Have everywhere about this land of Christ
In twelve great battles ruining overthrown.
And knowest thou now from whence I come—from him,
From waging bitter war with him; and he,   431
That did not shun to smite me in worse way,
Had yet that grace of courtesy in him left,
He spared to lift his hand against the King
Who made him knight: but many a knight was slain;
And many more and all his kith and kin   436
Clave to him, and abode in his own land.
And many more when Modred raised revolt,
Forgetful of their troth and fealty, clave
To Modred, and a remnant stays with me.   440
And of this remnant will I leave a part,
True men who love me still, for whom I live,
To guard thee in the wild hour coming on,
Lest but a hair of this low head be harm'd.
Fear not: thou shalt be guarded till my death.   445
Howbeit I know, if ancient prophecies
Have err'd not, that I march to meet my doom.
Thou hast not made my life so sweet to me,
That I the King should greatly care to live;
For thou hast spoilt the purpose of my life.   450
Bear with me for the last time while I show,
Even for thy sake, the sin which thou hast sinn'd
For when the Roman left us, and their law
Relax'd its hold upon us, and the ways
Were fill'd with rapine, here and there a deed   455
Of prowess done redress'd a random wrong.

But I was first of all the kings who drew
The knighthood-errant of this realm and all
The realms together under me, their Head,
In that fair Order of my Table Round,   460
A glorious company, the flower of men,
To serve as model for the mighty world,
And be the fair beginning of a time.
I made them lay their hands in mine and swear
To reverence the King, as if he were   465
Their conscience, and their conscience as their King,
To break the heathen and uphold the Christ,
To ride abroad redressing human wrongs,
To speak no slander, no, nor listen to it,
To honor his own word as if his God's,   470
To lead sweet lives in purest chastity,
To love one maiden only, cleave to her,
And worship her by years of noble deeds,
Until they won her; for indeed I knew
Of no more subtle master under heaven   475
Than is the maiden passion for a maid,
Not only to keep down the base in man,
But teach high thought, and amiable words
And courtliness, and the desire of fame,
And love of truth, and all that makes a man.   480
And all this throve before I wedded thee,
Believing, 'Lo, mine helpmate, one to feel
My purpose and rejoicing in my joy!'
Then came thy shameful sin with Lancelot;
Then came the sin of Tristram and Isolt;   485
Then others, following these my mightiest knights,

And drawing foul ensample from fair names,
Sinn'd also, till the loathsome opposite
Of all my heart had destined did obtain,
And all thro' thee! so that this life of mine   49
I guard as God's high gift from scathe and wrong,
Not greatly care to lose; but rather think
How sad it were for Arthur, should he live,
To sit once more within his lonely hall,
And miss the wonted number of my knights,   49
And miss to hear high talk of noble deeds
As in the golden days before thy sin.
For which of us who might be left could speak
Of the pure heart, nor seem to glance at thee?
And in thy bowers of Camelot or of Usk   50
Thy shadow still would glide from room to room,
And I should evermore be vext with thee
In hanging robe or vacant ornament,
Or ghostly footfall echoing on the stair.
For think not, tho' thou wouldst not love thy lord,   50
Thy lord has wholly lost his love for thee.
I am not made of so slight elements.
Yet must I leave thee, woman, to thy shame.
I hold that man the worst of public foes
Who either for his own or children's sake,   51
To save his blood from scandal, lets the wife
Whom he knows false abide and rule the house:
For being thro' his cowardice allow'd
Her station, taken everywhere for pure,
She like a new disease, unknown to men,   51
Creeps, no precaution used, among the crowd,

Makes wicked lightnings of her eyes, and saps
The fealty of our friends, and stirs the pulse
With devil's leaps, and poisons half the young.
Worst of the worst were that man he that reigns!   520
Better the King's waste hearth and aching heart
Than thou reseated in thy place of light,
The mockery of my people and their bane!"

He paused, and in the pause she crept an inch
Nearer, and laid her hands about his feet.   525
Far off a solitary trumpet blew.
Then waiting by the doors the war-horse neigh'd
As at a friend's voice, and he spake again:

"Yet think not that I come to urge thy crimes;
I did not come to curse thee, Guinevere,   530
I, whose vast pity almost makes me die
To see thee, laying there thy golden head,
My pride in happier summers, at my feet.
The wrath which forced my thoughts on that fierce law,
The doom of treason and the flaming death,—   535
When first I learnt thee hidden here,—is past.
The pang—which, while I weigh'd thy heart with one
Too wholly true to dream untruth in thee,
Made my tears burn—is also past—in part.
And all is past, the sin is sinn'd, and I,   540
Lo, I forgive thee, as Eternal God
Forgives! do thou for thine own soul the rest.
But how to take last leave of all I loved?
O golden hair, with which I used to play

Not knowing! O imperial-moulded form,   545
And beauty such as never woman wore,
Until it came a kingdom's curse with thee—
I cannot touch thy lips, they are not mine,
But Lancelot's; nay, they never were the King's.
I cannot take thy hand; that too is flesh,   550
And in the flesh thou hast sinn'd; and mine own flesh,
Here looking down on thine polluted, cries,
'I loathe thee': yet not less, O Guinevere,
For I was ever virgin save for thee,
My love thro' flesh hath wrought into my life   555
So far that my doom is, I love thee still.
Let no man dream but that I love thee still.
Perchance, and so thou purify thy soul,
And so thou lean on our fair father Christ,
Hereafter in that world where all are pure   560
We two may meet before high God, and thou
Wilt spring to me, and claim me thine, and know
I am thine husband—not a smaller soul,
Nor Lancelot, nor another. Leave me that,
I charge thee, my last hope. Now must I hence.   565
Thro' the thick night I hear the trumpet blow:
They summon me their King to lead mine hosts
Far down to that great battle in the west,
Where I must strike against the man they call
My sister's son—no kin of mine, who leagues   570
With Lords of the White Horse, heathen, and knights,
Traitors— and strike him dead, and meet myself
Death, or I know not what mysterious doom.
And thou remaining here wilt learn the event;

But hither shall I never come again,   575
Never lie by thy side, see thee no more—
Farewell!"

              And while she grovell'd at his feet,
She felt the King's breath wander o'er her neck,
And in the darkness o'er her fallen head
Perceived the waving of his hands that blest.   580

Then, listening till those armed steps were gone,
Rose the pale Queen, and in her anguish found
The casement: "peradventure," so she thought,
"If I might see his face, and not be seen."
And lo, he sat on horseback at the door!   585
And near him the sad nuns with each a light
Stood, and he gave them charge about the Queen,
To guard and foster her for evermore.
And while he spake to these his helm was lower'd,
To which for crest the golden dragon clung   590
Of Britain; so she did not see the face,
Which then was as an angel's, but she saw,
Wet with the mists and smitten by the lights,
The Dragon of the great Pendragonship
Blaze, making all the night a steam of fire.   595
And even then he turn'd; and more and more
The moony vapor rolling round the King,
Who seem'd the phantom of a giant in it,
Enwound him fold by fold, and made him gray
And grayer, till himself became as mist   600
Before her, moving ghostlike to his doom.

Then she stretch'd out her arms and cried aloud,
"O Arthur!" there her voice brake suddenly,
Then—as a stream that spouting from a cliff
Fails in mid air, but gathering at the base   605
Re-makes itself, and flashes down the vale—
Went on in passionate utterance:

                                   "Gone—my lord!
Gone thro' my sin to slay and to be slain!
And he forgave me, and I could not speak.
Farewell? I should have answer'd his farewell.   610
His mercy choked me. Gone, my lord the King,
My own true lord! how dare I call him mine?
The shadow of another cleaves to me,
And makes me one pollution: he, the King,
Call'd me polluted: shall I kill myself?   615
What help in that? I cannot kill my sin,
If soul be soul; nor can I kill my shame;
No, nor by living can I live it down.
The days will grow to weeks, the weeks to months,
The months will add themselves and make the years,   620
The years will roll into the centuries,
And mine will ever be a name of scorn.
I must not dwell on that defeat of fame.
Let the world be; that is but of the world—
What else? what hope? I think there was a hope,   625
Except he mock'd me when he spake of hope;
His hope he call'd it; but he never mocks,
For mockery is the fume of little hearts.
And blessed be the King, who hath forgiven

My wickedness to him, and left me hope 630
That in mine own heart I can live down sin
And be his mate hereafter in the heavens
Before high God! Ah great and gentle lord,
Who wast, as is the conscience of a saint
Among his warring senses, to thy knights— 635
To whom my false voluptuous pride, that took
Full easily all impressions from below,
Would not look up, or half-despised the height
To which I would not or I could not climb—
I thought I could not breathe in that fine air, 640
That pure severity of perfect light—
I yearn'd for warmth and color which I found
In Lancelot—now I see thee what thou art,
Thou art the highest and most human too,
Not Lancelot, nor another. Is there none 645
Will tell the King I love him tho' so late?
Now—ere he goes to the great battle? none:
Myself must tell him in that purer life,
But now it were too daring. Ah my God,
What might I not have made of thy fair world, 650
Had I but loved thy highest creature here?
It was my duty to have loved the highest;
It surely was my profit had I known;
It would have been my pleasure had I seen.
We needs must love the highest when we see it, 655
Not Lancelot, nor another."

                Here her hand
Grasp'd, made her vail her eyes: she look'd and saw

The novice, weeping, suppliant, and said to her,
"Yea, little maid, for am *I* not forgiven?"
Then glancing up beheld the holy nuns   660
All round her, weeping; and her heart was loosed
Within her, and she wept with these and said:

    "Ye know me then, that wicked one, who broke
The vast design and purpose of the King.
O, shut me round with narrowing nunnery-walls,   665
Meek maidens, from the voices crying, 'Shame!'
I must not scorn myself: he loves me still.
Let no one dream but that he loves me still.
So let me, if you do not shudder at me,
Nor shun to call me sister, dwell with you;   670
Wear black and white, and be a nun like you,
Fast with your fasts, not feasting with your feasts;
Grieve with your griefs, not grieving at your joys,
But not rejoicing; mingle with your rites;
Pray and be pray'd for; lie before your shrines;   675
Do each low office of your holy house;
Walk your dim cloister, and distribute dole
To poor sick people, richer in His eyes
Who ransom'd us, and haler too than I;
And treat their loathsome hurts and heal mine own;   680
And so wear out in alms-deed and in prayer
The sombre close of that voluptuous day
Which wrought the ruin of my lord the King."

    She said: they took her to themselves; and she
Still hoping, fearing "is it yet too late?"   685

Dwelt with them, till in time their abbess died.
Then she, for her good deeds and her pure life,
And for the power of ministration in her,
And likewise for the high rank she had borne,
Was chosen abbess, there, an abbess, lived   690
For three brief years, and there, an abbess, past
To where beyond these voices there is peace.

THE PASSING OF ARTHUR

THAT story which the bold Sir Bedivere,
First made and latest left of all the knights,
Told, when the man was no more than a voice
In the white winter of his age, to those
With whom he dwelt, new faces, other minds.   5

For on their march to westward, Bedivere,
Who slowly paced among the slumbering host,
Heard in his tent the moanings of the King:

"I found Him in the shining of the stars,
I mark'd Him in the flowering of His fields,   10
But in His ways with men I find Him not.
I waged His wars, and now I pass and die.
O me! for why is all around us here
As if some lesser god had made the world,
But had not force to shape it as he would   15
Till the High God behold it from beyond,
And enter it, and make it beautiful?
Or else as if the world were wholly fair,
But that these eyes of men are dense and dim,
And have not power to see it as it is: 20
Perchance, because we see not to the close;—
For I, being simple, thought to work His will,

And have but stricken with the sword in vain;
And all whereon I lean'd in wife and friend
Is traitor to my peace, and all my realm   25
Reels back into the beast, and is no more.
My God, thou hast forgotten me in my death:
Nay—God my Christ—I pass but shall not die."

   Then, ere that last weird battle in the west,
There came on Arthur sleeping, Gawain kill'd   30
In Lancelot's war, the ghost of Gawain blown
Along a wandering wind, and past his ear
Went shrilling: "Hollow, hollow all delight!
Hail, King! to-morrow thou shalt pass away.
Farewell! there is an isle of rest for thee.   35
And I am blown along a wandering wind,
And hollow, hollow, hollow all delight!"
And fainter onward, like wild birds that change
Their season in the night and wail their way
From cloud to cloud, down the long wind the dream   40
Shrill'd; but in going mingled with dim cries
Far in the moonlit haze among the hills,
As of some lonely city sack'd by night,
When all is lost, and wife and child with wail
Pass to new lords; and Arthur woke and call'd: 45
"Who spake? A dream. O light upon the wind,
Thine, Gawain, was the voice—are these dim
    cries
Thine? or doth all that haunts the waste and
    wild
Mourn, knowing it will go along with me?"

This heard the bold Sir Bedivere and spake: 50
"O me, my King, let pass whatever will,
Elves, and the harmless glamour of the field;
But in their stead thy name and glory cling
To all high places like a golden cloud
For ever: but as yet thou shalt not pass.   55
Light was Gawain in life, and light in death
Is Gawain, for the ghost is as the man;
And care not thou for dreams from him, but rise—
I hear the steps of Modred in the west,
And with him many of thy people, and knights   60
Once thine, whom thou hast loved, but grosser grown
Than heathen, spitting at their vows and thee.
Right well in heart they know thee for the King.
Arise, go forth and conquer as of old."

Then spake King Arthur to Sir Bedivere: 65
"Far other is this battle in the west
Whereto we move than when we strove in youth,
And brake the petty kings, and fought with Rome,
Or thrust the heathen from the Roman wall,
And shook him thro' the north. Ill doom is mine   70
To war against my people and my knights.
The king who fights his people fights himself.
And they my knights, who loved me once, the stroke
That strikes them dead is as my death to me.
Yet let us hence, and find or feel a way   75
Thro' this blind haze which, ever since I saw
One lying in the dust at Almesbury,
Hath folded in the passes of the world."

Then rose the King and moved his host by
    night,
And ever push'd Sir Modred, league by league,   80
Back to the sunset bound of Lyonnesse—
A land of old upheaven from the abyss
By fire, to sink into the abyss again;
Where fragments of forgotten peoples dwelt,
And the long mountains ended in a coast   85
Of ever-shifting sand, and far away
The phantom circle of a moaning sea.
There the pursuer could pursue no more,
And he that fled no further fly the King;
And there, that day when the great light of heaven 90
Burn'd at his lowest in the rolling year,
On the waste sand by the waste sea they closed.
Nor ever yet had Arthur fought a fight
Like this last, dim, weird battle of the west.
A death-white mist slept over sand and sea,   95
Whereof the chill, to him who breathed it, drew
Down with his blood, till all his heart was cold
With formless fear; and even on Arthur fell
Confusion, since he saw not whom he fought.
For friend and foe were shadows in the mist,   100
And friend slew friend not knowing whom he slew;
And some had visions out of golden youth,
And some beheld the faces of old ghosts
Look in upon the battle; and in the mist
Was many a noble deed, many a base,   105
And chance and craft and strength in single fights,
And ever and anon with host to host

Shocks, and the splintering spear, the hard mail hewn,
Shield-breakings, and the clash of brands, the crash
Of battle-axes on shatter'd helms, and shrieks   110
After the Christ, of those who falling down
Look'd up for heaven, and only saw the mist;
And shouts of heathen and the traitor knights,
Oaths, insult, filth, and monstrous blasphemies,
Sweat, writhings, anguish, laboring of the lungs   115
In that close mist, and cryings for the light,
Moans of the dying, and voices of the dead.

　Last, as by some one deathbed after wail
Of suffering, silence follows, or thro' death
Or death-like swoon, thus over all that shore,   120
Save for some whisper of the seething seas,
A dead hush fell; but when the dolorous day
Grew drearier toward twilight falling, came
A bitter wind, clear from the north, and blew
The mist aside, and with that wind the tide   125
Rose, and the pale King glanced across the field
Of battle: but no man was moving there;
Nor any cry of Christian heard thereon,
Nor yet of heathen; only the wan wave
Brake in among dead faces, to and fro   130
Swaying the helpless hands, and up and down
Tumbling the hollow helmets of the fallen,
And shiver'd brands that once had fought with
　　　Rome,
And rolling far along the gloomy shores
The voice of days of old and days to be.   135

Then spake King Arthur to Sir Bedivere,
And whiter than the mist that all day long
Had held the field of battle was the King:

"Hearest thou this great voice that shakes the world,
And wastes the narrow realm whereon we move,   140
And beats upon the faces of the dead,
My dead, as tho' they had not died for me?—
O Bedivere, for on my heart hath fallen
Confusion, till I know not what I am,
Nor whence I am, nor whether I be king;   145
Behold, I seem but king among the dead."

Then spake the bold Sir Bedivere: "My King;
King everywhere! and so the dead have kings,
There also will I worship thee as king.
Yet still thy life is whole, and still I live   150
Who love thee; but who hates thee, he that brought
The heathen back among us, yonder stands,
Modred, unharm'd, the traitor of thine house."

Then spake the King: "My house hath been my
     doom.
But call not thou this traitor of my house   155
Who hath but dwelt beneath one roof with me.
My house are rather they who sware my vows,
Yea, even while they brake them, own'd me king.
And well for thee, saying in my dark hour,
When all the purport of my throne hath fail'd,   160
That quick or dead thou holdest me for king.

King am I, whatsoever be their cry;
And one last act of kinghood shalt thou see
Yet, ere I pass." And uttering this the King
Made at the man: then Modred smote his liege   165
Hard on that helm which many a heathen sword
Had beaten thin; while Arthur at one blow,
Striking the last stroke with Excalibur,
Slew him, and, all but slain himself, he fell.

So all day long the noise of battle roll'd   170
Among the mountains by the winter sea;
Until King Arthur's Table, man by man,
Had fallen in Lyonnesse about their lord,
King Arthur. Then, because his wound was deep,
The bold Sir Bedivere uplifted him,   175
And bore him to a chapel nigh the field,
A broken chancel with a broken cross,
That stood on a dark strait of barren land:
On one side lay the Ocean, and on one
Lay a great water, and the moon was full.   180

Then spake King Arthur to Sir Bedivere:
"The sequel of to-day unsolders all
The goodliest fellowship of famous knights
Whereof this world holds record. Such a sleep
They sleep—the men I loved. I think that we   185
Shall never more, at any future time,
Delight our souls with talk of knightly deeds,
Walking about the gardens and the halls
Of Camelot, as in the days that were.

I perish by this people which I made,— 190
Tho' Merlin sware that I should come again
To rule once more; but, let what will be be,
I am so deeply smitten thro' the helm
That without help I cannot last till morn.
Thou therefore take my brand Excalibur, 195
Which was my pride: for thou rememberest how
In those old days, one summer noon, an arm
Rose up from out the bosom of the lake,
Clothed in white samite, mystic, wonderful,
Holding the sword—and how I row'd across 200
And took it, and have worn it, like a king;
And, wheresoever I am sung or told
In aftertime, this also shall be known.
But now delay not: take Excalibur,
And fling him far into the middle mere; 205
Watch what thou seest, and lightly bring me word."

    To him replied the bold Sir Bedivere:
"It is not meet, Sir King, to leave thee thus,
Aidless, alone, and smitten thro' the helm—
A little thing may harm a wounded man; 210
Yet I thy hest will all perform at full,
Watch what I see, and lightly bring thee word."

    So saying, from the ruin'd shrine he stept,
And in the moon athwart the place of tombs,
Where lay the mighty bones of ancient men, 215
Old knights, and over them the sea-wind sang
Shrill, chill, with flakes of foam. He, stepping down

By zigzag paths and juts of pointed rock,
Came on the shining levels of the lake.

There drew he forth the brand Excalibur,   220
And o'er him, drawing it, the winter moon,
Brightening the skirts of a long cloud, ran forth
And sparkled keen with frost against the hilt;
For all the haft twinkled with diamond sparks,
Myriads of topaz-lights, and jacinth-work   225
Of subtlest jewellery. He gazed so long
That both his eyes were dazzled as he stood,
This way and that dividing the swift mind,
In act to throw: but at the last it seem'd
Better to leave Excalibur conceal'd   230
There in the many-knotted water-flags,
That whistled stiff and dry about the marge.
So strode he back slow to the wounded King.

Then spake King Arthur to Sir Bedivere:
"Hast thou perform'd my mission which I gave?   235
What is it thou hast seen? or what hast heard?"

And answer made the bold Sir Bedivere:
"I heard the ripple washing in the reeds,
And the wild water lapping on the crag."

To whom replied King Arthur, faint and pale: 240
"Thou hast betray'd thy nature and thy name,
Not rendering true answer, as beseem'd
Thy fealty, nor like a noble knight;

For surer sign had follow'd, either hand,
Or voice, or else a motion of the mere.   245
This is a shameful thing for men to lie.
Yet now, I charge thee, quickly go again,
As thou art lief and dear, and do the thing
I bade thee, watch, and lightly bring me word."

    Then went Sir Bedivere the second time   250
Across the ridge, and paced beside the mere,
Counting the dewy pebbles, fixt in thought;
But when he saw the wonder of the hilt,
How curiously and strangely chased, he smote
His palms together, and he cried aloud: 255

    "And if indeed I cast the brand away,
Surely a precious thing, one worthy note,
Should thus be lost for ever from the earth,
Which might have pleased the eyes of many men.
What good should follow this, if this were done?   260
What harm, undone? Deep harm to disobey,
Seeing obedience is the bond of rule.
Were it well to obey then, if a king demand
An act unprofitable, against himself?
The King is sick, and knows not what he does.   265
What record or what relic of my lord
Should be to aftertime, but empty breath
And rumors of a doubt? But were this kept,
Stored in some treasure-house of mighty kings,
Some one might show it at a joust of arms,   270
Saying: 'King Arthur's sword, Excalibur,

Wrought by the lonely Maiden of the Lake.
Nine years she wrought it, sitting in the deeps
Upon the hidden bases of the hills.'
So might some old man speak in the aftertime   275
To all the people, winning reverence.
But now much honor and much fame were lost."

So spake he, clouded with his own conceit,
And hid Excalibur the second time,
And so strode back slow to the wounded King.   280

Then spoke King Arthur, breathing heavily:
"What is it thou hast seen? or what hast heard?"

And answer made the bold Sir Bedivere:
"I heard the water lapping on the crag,
And the long ripple washing in the reeds."   285

To whom replied King Arthur, much in wrath:
"Ah miserable, and unkind, untrue,
Unknightly, traitor-hearted! Woe is me!
Authority forgets a dying king,
Laid widow'd of the power in his eye   290
That bow'd the will. I see thee what thou art,
For thou, the latest-left of all my knights,
In whom should meet the offices of all,
Thou wouldst betray me for the precious hilt;
Either from lust of gold, or like a girl   295
Valuing the giddy pleasure of the eyes.
Yet, for a man may fail in duty twice,

And the third time may prosper, get thee hence:
But, if thou spare to fling Excalibur,
I will arise and slay thee with my hands." 300

Then quickly rose Sir Bedivere, and ran,
And, leaping down the ridges lightly, plunged
Among the bulrush beds, and clutch'd the sword,
And strongly wheel'd and threw it. The great brand
Made lightnings in the splendor of the moon, 305
And flashing round and round, and whirl'd in an arch,
Shot like a streamer of the northern morn,
Seen where the moving isles of winter shock
By night, with noises of the Northern Sea.
So flash'd and fell the brand Excalibur; 310
But ere he dipt the surface, rose an arm
Clothed in white samite, mystic, wonderful,
And caught him by the hilt, and brandish'd him
Three times, and drew him under in the mere.
And lightly went the other to the King. 315

Then spoke King Arthur, drawing thicker breath:
"Now see I by thine eyes that this is done.
Speak out: what is it thou hast heard, or seen?"

And answer made the bold Sir Bedivere:
"Sir King, I closed mine eyelids, lest the gems 320
Should blind my purpose, for I never saw,
Nor shall see, here or elsewhere, till I die,
Not tho' I live three lives of mortal men,
So great a miracle as yonder hilt.

Then with both hands I flung him, wheeling him;   325
But when I look'd again, behold an arm,
Clothed in white samite, mystic, wonderful,
That caught him by the hilt, and brandish'd him
Three times, and drew him under in the mere."

And answer made King Arthur, breathing hard: 330
"My end draws nigh; 't is time that I were gone.
Make broad thy shoulders to receive my weight,
And bear me to the margin; yet I fear
My wound hath taken cold, and I shall die."

So saying, from the pavement he half rose,   335
Slowly, with pain, reclining on his arm,
And looking wistfully with wide blue eyes
As in a picture.   Him Sir Bedivere
Remorsefully regarded thro' his tears,
And would have spoken, but he found not words;   340
Then took with care, and kneeling on one knee,
O'er both his shoulders drew the languid hands,
And rising bore him thro' the place of tombs.

But, as he walk'd, King Arthur panted hard,
Like one that feels a nightmare on his bed   345
When all the house is mute. So sigh'd the King,
Muttering and murmuring at his ear, "Quick, quick!
I fear it is too late, and I shall die."
But the other swiftly strode from ridge to ridge,
Clothed with his breath, and looking, as he walk'd,   350
Larger than human on the frozen hills.

He heard the deep behind him, and a cry
Before. His own thought drove him like a goad.
Dry clash'd his harness in the icy caves
And barren chasms, and all to left and right   355
The bare black cliff clang'd round him, as he based
His feet on juts of slippery crag that rang
Sharp-smitten with the dint of armed heels—
And on a sudden, lo, the level lake,
And the long glories of the winter moon!   360

Then saw they how there hove a dusky barge,
Dark as a funeral scarf from stem to stern,
Beneath them; and descending they were ware
That all the decks were dense with stately forms,
Black-stoled, black-hooded, like a dream—by these 365
Three queens with crowns of gold: and from them
    rose
A cry that shiver'd to the tingling stars,
And, as it were one voice, an agony
Of lamentation, like a wind that shrills
All night in a waste land, where no one comes,   370
Or hath come, since the making of the world.

Then murmur'd Arthur, "Place me in the barge."
So to the barge they came. There those three
    queens
Put forth their hands, and took the King, and wept.
But she that rose the tallest of them all   375
And fairest laid his head upon her lap,
And loosed the shatter'd casque, and chafed his hands,

And call'd him by his name, complaining loud,
And dropping bitter tears against a brow
Striped with dark blood: for all his face was white   380
And colorless, and like the wither'd moon
Smote by the fresh beam of the springing east;
And all his greaves and cuisses dash'd with drops
Of onset; and the light and lustrous curls—
That made his forehead like a rising sun   385
High from the daïs-throne—were parch'd with dust,
Or, clotted into points and hanging loose,
Mixt with the knightly growth that fringed his lips.
So like a shatter'd column lay the King;
Not like that Arthur who, with lance in rest,   390
From spur to plume a star of tournament,
Shot thro' the lists at Camelot, and charged
Before the eyes of ladies and of kings.

   Then loudly cried the bold Sir Bedivere:
"Ah! my Lord Arthur, whither shall I go?   395
Where shall I hide my forehead and my eyes?
For now I see the true old times are dead,
When every morning brought a noble chance,
And every chance brought out a noble knight.
Such times have been not since the light that led   400
The holy Elders with the gift of myrrh.
But now the whole Round Table is dissolved
Which was an image of the mighty world,
And I, the last, go forth companionless,
And the days darken round me, and the years,   405
Among new men, strange faces, other minds."

And slowly answer'd Arthur from the barge:
"The old order changeth, yielding place to new
And God fulfils himself in many ways,
Lest one good custom should corrupt the world.   410
Comfort thyself: what comfort is in me?
I have lived my life, and that which I have done
May He within himself make pure! but thou,
If thou shouldst never see my face again,
Pray for my soul. More things are wrought by
          prayer   41[
Than this world dreams of. Wherefore, let thy voice
Rise like a fountain for me night and day.
For what are men better than sheep or goats
That nourish a blind life within the brain,
If, knowing God, they lift not hands of prayer   420
Both for themselves and those who call them friend?
For so the whole round earth is every way
Bound by gold chains about the feet of God.
But now farewell. I am going a long way
With these thou seest—if indeed I go—   425
For all my mind is clouded with a doubt—
To the island-valley of Avilion;
Where falls not hail, or rain, or any snow,
Nor ever wind blows loudly; but it lies
Deep-meadow'd, happy, fair with orchard lawns   430
And bowery hollows crown'd with summer sea,
Where I will heal me of my grievous wound."

So said he, and the barge with oar and sail
Moved from the brink, like some full-breasted swan

That, fluting a wild carol ere her death,   43.
Ruffles her pure cold plume, and takes the flood
With swarthy webs.   Long stood Sir Bedivere
Revolving many memories, till the hull
Look'd one black dot against the verge of dawn,
And on the mere the wailing died away.   440

But when that moan had past for evermore,
The stillness of the dead world's winter dawn
Amazed him, and he groan'd, "The King is gone."
And therewithal came on him the weird rhyme,
"From the great deep to the great deep he goes."   445

Whereat he slowly turn'd and slowly clomb
The last hard footstep of that iron crag,
Thence mark'd the black hull moving yet, and cried:
"He passes to be king among the dead,
And after healing of his grievous wound   450
He comes again; but—if he come no more—
O me, be yon dark queens in yon black boat,
Who shriek'd and wail'd, the three whereat we gazed
On that high day, when, clothed with living light,
They stood before his throne in silence, friends   455
Of Arthur, who should help him at his need?"

Then from the dawn it seem'd there came, but faint
As from beyond the limit of the world,
Like the last echo born of a great cry,
Sounds, as if some fair city were one voice   460
Around a king returning from his wars.

Thereat once more he moved about, and clomb
Even to the highest he could climb, and saw,
Straining his eyes beneath an arch of hand,
Or thought he saw, the speck that bare the King,   465
Down that long water opening on the deep
Somewhere far off, pass on and on, and go
From less to less and vanish into light.
And the new sun rose bringing the new year.

NOTES

THE COMING OF ARTHUR

23, 5–19. **Ere Arthur came,** etc. See " The Arthurian Legend," Introduction, p. 8.

24, 39. **Brake.** See Glossary, p. 208, for obsolete words and unusual meanings. What is the subject of *brake?*

27, 111–115. **Carâdos,** etc. For names of the revolting kings, see Malory, Book I, Chap. 10. Chapters 11–15 tell of the battle.

28, 150. **Merlin.** Merlin is the sage of Arthur's court, the type of earthly wisdom. Read the Idyll, " Merlin and Vivien."

166. **Cuckoo chased,** etc. The cuckoo deposits her eggs in the nests of other birds.

32, 261. **Vows.** Cf. " Guinevere," 464–480. These lines are referred to frequently. They state the ideals of Arthur's order and are well worth memorizing. For method of memorizing, see Introduction, p. 18.

266–308. The allegorical meaning of the Idylls has been much discussed. The young student should approach this phase of the work with a mind alert to grasp the deeper meaning, and at the same time free from a subserviency that would compel him to accept ready-made the conclusions of teachers or of commentators. One point should be kept clearly in mind: the allegory is not always consistent. Tennyson himself, when pressed for an explanation of the " three fair queens " (1.275, also G. L., 225), said: " They mean that [Faith, Hope, and Charity] and they do not. They are also three of the noblest women. They are also those three Graces, but they are much more. I hate to be tied down to say, ' *this* means *that*,' because the thought within the image is much more than any one interpretation." —*Memoir, II,* 127.

In general, it is more satisfactory to consider the characters of the poem as men and women, to recognize whatever spiritual significance may be evident in their actions, and to discern the applications of their triumphs and defeats to the world in which we live. In *The Poetry of Tennyson*, Dr. Henry Van Dyke writes:

" We must distinguish, then, between the allegorical fragments which Tennyson has woven into his work, and the substance of the Idylls; between the scenery and mechanical appliances, and the actors who move upon the stage. The attempt to interpret the poem as a strict allegory breaks down at once and spoils the story. Suppose you say that Arthur is the Conscience, and Guinevere is the Flesh, and Merlin is the Intellect; then, pray what is Lancelot, and what is Geraint, and what is Vivien? What business has the Conscience to fall in love with the Flesh? What attraction has Vivien for the Intellect without any passions? If Merlin is not a man, '*Que diable allait-il faire dans cette galère?*' The whole affair becomes absurd, unreal, incomprehensible, uninteresting.

"But when we take the King and his people as actual men and women, when we put ourselves into the story and let it carry us along, then we understand that it is a parable; that is to say, it casts beside itself an image, a reflection, of something spiritual, just as a man walking in the sunlight is followed by his shadow. It is a tale of human life, and therefore, being told with a purpose, it

Shadows Sense at war with Soul.

"Let us take up this idea of the conflict between sense and soul and carry it out through the Idylls."

For an excellent allegorical interpretation of "The Coming of Arthur," see Stopford Brooke: *Tennyson, His Art and Relation to Modern Life*, p. 259 ff., also the Rolfe Edition, *Idylls of the King*, p. 183 ff. See also "The Allegory," Introduction, p. 16.

33, 282. Lady of the Lake. See note on L. E., 212–226.

36, 362. Fairy changeling. "The elves that fairies were supposed to leave in exchange for the human babies they stole, could sometimes be recognized as *changelings* by their shrivelled and shrunken appearance."—Rolfe Edition, *Idylls of the King*.

373–5. A ship, etc. Compare the ship which carries the King away in "The Passing of Arthur." This account of the coming of Arthur, together with Merlin's speech ending with line 410, suggests "the deep and favorite thought of Tennyson of the pre-existence of the soul." Read the splendid passage in Wordsworth's "Ode on Intimations of Immortality," beginning:

<blockquote>
Our birth is but a sleep and a forgetting:
The Soul that rises with us, our Life's Star,
Hath had elsewhere its setting,
And cometh from afar.
</blockquote>

37, 402–410. Rain, rain, etc. Cf. note on G. L., 280–87. The following interpretation is given by Pallen:

" Life has its many vicissitudes, its rain and its sunshine,
storm and calm, hopes and fears, joys and sorrows, but truth
abides unchanging, whether it be clothed or naked to human
eyes. The soul, which is the house of truth, passes through all
changes of time, all vicissitudes of space, from eternity to eternity."—*The Meaning of the Idylls of the King*, p. 33.

38, 421. **Again to come.** " Yet some men yet say in many
parts of England that king Arthur is not dead, but had by the
will of our Lord Jesu in another place. And men say that he
shall come again, and he shall win the holy cross. I will not say
it shall be so, but rather I will say, here in this world he changed
his life. But men say that there is written on his tomb this verse.

**𝔥ic iacet Arthurus Rex quondam
Rexque futurus.**
MALORY, XXI, 7.

There have been many similar beliefs in the return of great national heroes, for example, Charlemagne, Barbarossa, and Tell.

39, 450. **Then was latter April.** See note on the year-cycle
of the Idylls, " Guinevere," p. 203.

481–501. **Blow trumpet,** etc. " Lastly, as a piece of glorious
literature, there is the marriage and coronation song of the
knights. It was not in the first draft of ' The Coming of Arthur.'
It embodies the thought of the poem, grips the whole meaning
of it together. And its sound is the sound of martial triumph, of
victorious weapons in battle, and of knights in arms. We hear
in the carefully varied chorus, in the very rattle and shattering
of the vowels in the words, the beating of axe on helm and shaft
on shield. Rugged, clanging, clashing lines . . . it is a splendid effort of art. King Olaf might have sung it."—STOPFORD
BROOKE.

GARETH AND LYNETTE

43, 1. **Bellicent** is Arthur's sister. See her testimony concerning him in " The Coming of Arthur," 253–423.

3. **Spate.** See Glossary for obsolete words and unusual meanings.

17–25. **A worse were better,** etc. These lines should be memorized. Gareth is a type of noble idealism. As you proceed,
mark passages that show this quality. What were his ideals, and
how far did they affect his actions?

44, 25. **Gawain** and **Modred** are Gareth's brothers. The

name *Gawain* is accented on either syllable as the meter demands.
See "The Passing of Arthur," 56–7.

46. **Book of Hours.** A book of prayers for various hours.
Such books were often profusely illuminated.

45, 66. Brand Excalibur. King Arthur's Sword, called *brand*
from its flashing. See "The Coming of Arthur," 295–304.

62–65. Gold, etc. Interpret these lines. What do the gold
and steel stand for respectively in Gareth's mind?

46, 76. Barons' war. See "The Coming of Arthur," 62–73,
100–123.

85. Give the syntax of *thee* and of *jousts* and *wars*.

89. **Frights.** A noun in apposition with *shocks* and *tourney
falls*.

115–118. Memorize. Read aloud so as to bring out Gareth's
meaning.

47, 119. Many who deem him not, etc. Many doubted
Arthur's royal descent. See "The Coming of Arthur," 177–236.

48, 141. Who. The personal pronoun immediately preced-
ing a relative is often omitted by Tennyson.

49, 173–4. Waken'd by the wind, etc. Cf. *In Memoriam*,
XCV, last three stanzas.

50, 185. Camelot is probably the site of Queen-Camel in
Somerset. Efforts to localize scenes of *The Idylls of the King*,
however, are generally not worth while.

"There is not one touch of the real world in all the scenery
that Tennyson invents in his poem. It belongs throughout to
that country which eye hath not seen nor ear heard, but which
the heart of man has imagined."—STOPFORD A. BROOKE.

"Of course Camelot for instance, a city of Shadowy Palaces,
is everywhere symbolic of the gradual growth of human beliefs
and institutions, and of the spiritual development of man."—
TENNYSON, *Memoir II*, 127.

51, 212–226. The Lady of the Lake symbolizes Religion.

"The forms of the church are forever changing and flowing
like water, but her great arms are stretched out immovable like
the cross."

The drops of water represent baptism; the sword represents
the spiritual weapons of the soul; and the censer, "human prayer
and sacrifice." The fish was a symbol of the early Christians;
Arthur's wars center around Religion, and typify the endless
conflict between good and evil. For the **three queens** (l. 225),
see note on the allegory, C. A., 266–308.

222. **Time were nothing.** The war of the soul centering in
Religion is eternal.

52, 238–47. Is this the truth?

248–74. Gareth's followers represent those who believe nothing but their senses; the King here symbolizes the Soul; and the city symbolizes moral and spiritual culture, qualities beyond the comprehension of the mere senses. The fairy kings and queens, possibly symbolizing science and art, came from the East. Merlin holds with the idealists that the King, the Soul, is the only reality, and urges that men shall bind themselves by spiritual vows, vows impossible to keep because they represent ideals, which always rise beyond any present attainment. If they are unwilling to take these vows, let them remain outside the spiritual city, " among the cattle of the field." The city, built to the music of this divine harmony, is never completed, although constantly in process of construction.

Do you expect Gareth to take the vows or remain outside among the cattle? Why?

249–51. I have seen, etc. To what optical illusion does Merlin refer?

53, 266. Vows. By all means memorize " Guinevere," 464–480.

280–87. Riddling of the Bards. Cf. " The Coming of Arthur," 402–10, also the note on same. Merlin is purposely unintelligible. The truth seems mockery to you because you do not understand it. Gareth must accept some things on faith. Idealism is often incompatible with the scientific spirit of doubt which demands proof. Oracles are notoriously vague. Compare the prophesy that Athens should find safety in her wooden walls.

54, 308–9. The Idyll, " Gareth and Lynette," portrays the court before the sin of Lancelot and Guinevere has corrupted the social order. Cf. 320–25. Lines 310–430 show the justice of the King. See " The Theme of the Idylls," Introduction, p. 15.

56, 367. Aurelius Emrys, Uther, former kings. Cf. " The Coming of Arthur," 13–19.

58, 400. Rose. What is its subject?

419. Churl. Cf. *In Memoriam*, CXI.

59, 444–5. Wan-sallow, root-bitten. Note Tennyson's descriptive compounds. Cf. *long-vaulted*, 312, *high-arching over-browed the hearth*, 400.

451. Lancelot. King Arthur's chief knight.

> Whereat the two,
> For each had warded either in the fight,
> Sware on the field of death a deathless love.
> And Arthur said, Man's word is God in man:
> Let chance what will, I trust thee to the death.
> "The Coming of Arthur," 129–33.

60, 465. **Sir Fair-hands.** The English meaning of Beaumains, which was Malory's nickname for Gareth.

473.   What innate dissimilarity of spirit is there between Kay and Gareth? Are they types of real people?

61, 490. **Caer-Eryri.** Snowdon. The line refers to another legend concerning the birth of Arthur.

492. **Isle Avilion.** The earthly paradise of the Britons; literally, island of apples.

62, 528. **Peter's knee.** Cf. *Matthew*, XVI, 18–19.

63, 557–9.   What is Arthur's ideal? Does Gareth need the admonition?

64, 579–608.   What characteristics are revealed by Lynette's words?

65, 586. **Best blood.** The sacramental wine.

66, 632–7.   Why does not Gareth assert his rank?

67, 665. **This . . . that.** Adjective pronouns. One servant bore a blank shield and helmet, the other held the horse and spear.

68, 692. **Bound.** Give the syntax.

69, 697–9. **Belike,** etc. To whom does Kay refer in these lines?

720–34.   Is Lynette a "snob"? Wherein are her standards different from those of an American girl?

72, 771. **Spit.** See Glossary. Why does Lynette use this word?

73, 805–7. **But at night,** etc. An allusion to the superstition that ghosts were permitted to "walk the night." Give parallels.

811. **For the deed's sake,** etc. Cf. Ruskin's discussion of "Advancement in Life" in the first part of *Sesame and Lilies.*

74, 829. **Peacock.** Often served at splendid feasts. When it was served, "all the guests took a solemn vow; the knights vowing bravery, and the ladies engaging to be loving and faithful."—STANLEY, *History of Birds*, quoted by Rolfe.

76, 884. **River.** In the allegory the river typifies time; Sir Morning Star, the temptations of youth.

899. **See that he fall,** etc.   What covert insult to Gareth is there in these lines?

79, 971.   Lynette's songs are interesting examples of feminine self-contradiction. While they reveal to the reader a change in her feelings toward her valiant champion, she intensifies the bitterness of her upbraidings.

80, 1002–6. **The flower that blows,** etc. What flower does he mean? What significance has its color?

1005–7. **Gareth's eyes had flying blots,** etc. Cf.

And on the splendor came, flashing me blind;
And seemed to me to be the Lord of all the world,
Being so huge.
"The Holy Grail," 413–15.

What is the allegorical significance of the golden shield and of the battle fought in mid stream?

81, 1032–57. What half conscious argument is Lynette holding with herself?

82, 1039. **Perchance.** Perchance what?

83, 1067. **Harden'd skins.** The hardened skins are the habits of a lifetime. See 1100–4. Trace out as much of the allegory as you can from the hint in the note to l. 884.

85, 1117. **Loud Southwesterns,** etc. This is one of Tennyson's marvelous pictures of nature. Mark and memorize others as you find them.

" As the showers descend from heaven to return to it in vapour, so Mr. Tennyson's loving observation of Nature and his muse seem to have had a compact of reciprocity well kept on both sides."—W. E. GLADSTONE, *London Quarterly Review,* Oct., 1859.

1133–41. Is your attitude toward Lynette changed by these lines?

86, 1163. **Comb.** A bowl-shaped hollow or valley inclosed on all sides but one by steep cliffs.—*Century Dictionary.*

87, 1172. **Vexillary.** Standard bearer. This passage refers to inscriptions on the cliffs near the river Gelt.

1175. **Five figures.** Possibly the senses. Why?

1179. **The hermit's cave.** What does the hermit's cave mean, and why does man seek shelter there? This passage states broadly the theme of the Idylls.

88, 1199–1202. What is the dramatic purpose of Gareth's announcement of his name and rank?

1210–14. Analyze for clause structure and then read aloud so as to bring out the meaning. What is the subject of *had sent* in l. 1213?

91, 1286–88. Cf. 1263–5. Why does Lynette wish the change to be made?

92, 1323–50. What makes the last knight so much more terrible than the others? Judging by this passage and by the remainder of this Idyll, what do you think was Tennyson's idea of death?

95, 1392. **He that told,** etc. Sir Thomas Malory. See his *Morte D'Arthur,* Bk. VII, 34 and 35.

1394. **He that told it later.** Tennyson. Which version do you prefer?

LANCELOT AND ELAINE

97. What change is coming over Elaine as portrayed in the first twenty-seven lines?

100, 92. Urged. What is the subject?

101, 121–35. Is there any excuse for Guinevere's feelings toward her husband?

132. He is all fault, etc. Cf.

> Faultily faultless, icily regular, splendid null,
> Dead perfection, no more.
> > *Maude*, I, 82–3.

102, 157. They prove to him his work. Cf. l. 129. Note Guinevere's allusions to Arthur's great life work and determine her attitude to it. In all of Guinevere's criticism of Arthur, what do you think is the one fault she feels most keenly? What really is the trouble with the King? Has she a right to complain?

103, 163. Lost in fancy. Can you suggest any of Lancelot's possible fancies?

105, 235. Full courtly, yet not falsely. Explain.

236–40. If what is fair, etc. Explain his meaning. Is this compliment or flattery?

242. Won by the mellow voice. Is the voice an index of character and culture? Watch some of the people you know best for your answer.

244–59. What difference between the moral and spiritual condition of Lancelot and the one who "had been the sleeker for it?"

106, 262. Not with half disdain, etc. Did you ever see illustration of *half disdain?* Compare Gawain's attitude in 642 ff.

270. Suddenly speaking. Why does Lancelot change the subject?

107, 279. Badon hill. Possibly in Dorsetshire. The location is uncertain. This is the only one of the battles authenticated by history.

"It is certain that a victory of the Britons at Mount Badon in the year 520 not only checked the progress of the West-Saxons, but was followed by a general pause in the English advance."— J. R. GREEN.

297. Wild White Horse. The emblem of the Saxon invaders.

108, 314–316. The fire of God.

> "Sir and my liege," he cried: "the fire of God
> Descends upon thee in the battle-field:
> I know thee for my King."

Said by Lancelot, " The Coming of Arthur," 127–9.

329–37. His face before her lived, etc. This passage was suggested to Tennyson by the ideal of a true portrait painter expressed by George Frederick Watts in a conversation with the poet. Watts's painting of Sir Galahad is one of the best known illustrations connected with the Idylls.

110, 380–2. Has Elaine a right to hope that Lancelot wears her favor for any other reason than for the perfection of his own disguise?

112, 422. Pendragon. A title conferred upon British chiefs in times of great danger, when they were invested with dictatorial powers. A golden dragon was the symbol. Cf. l. 432.

423. Mysteriously. Referring to the stories of Arthur's origin, and to the prophecies of his destiny:

> Tho' men may wound him that he will not die,
> But pass, again to come.
>
> "The Coming of Arthur," 421–2.

430. Clear-faced. Can you suggest a reason for this particular epithet here?

113, 453. Held the lists. The knights of the Round Table acted as a defensive party against all comers. Cf. the tournament at Ashby in *Ivanhoe*.

454–458. See Introduction, p. 13.

114, 480–84. As a wild wave, etc. Note Tennyson's allusions to the sea. Cf. G. L., 1117–19.

119, 617. He won. Who says this?

619. What is indicated by the different ways in which Guinevere and Elaine receive the news of Lancelot's wound?

640. Note the philosophical nature of his conclusions; contrast with Lancelot at Astolat, 260–68.

120, 642–6. He set himself to play upon her, etc. Cf. 260–4.

648. Loyal. Why does Elaine use this word?

666. Does Elaine, with a woman's intuition, detect the insincerity of Gawain's attentions, or is she innocently unconscious of his flirtatious wooing?

121, 677. Whom he loves. Why does not Elaine follow up this hint?

122, 706–9. Did Gawain really believe that he was doing an honorable thing in relinquishing the quest? Write a character sketch of some man you know of the Gawain type.

710–13. How much effect has the King's rebuke on Gawain?

123, 726. **She.** Who?

728. **Marr'd.** What is the subject of this verb?

734. **Smiled at each other.** What is the significance of these words?

126, 831–37. What is Lancelot's attitude toward Elaine's love? Ought he to have sent her away?

· 128, 871–2. **Honor rooted in dishonor,** etc. A Tennysonian paradox. True to whom? Why falsely true?

129, 923. Explain the meaning of the line.

132, 991–96. What is poetry? If it cannot be defined, it at least can be illustrated by such passages as this. The pupil should mark them, and read them aloud until they are peculiarly his own. Concerning memorizing, see Introduction, p. 18.

1000–11. Tennyson's muse is essentially lyric. Nowhere in literature, not even excepting Shakespeare, are there more beautiful "drops of song" interspersed in longer works. Every student should read the lyrics in *The Princess.* E. C. Stedman says of them:

"The songs, added in the second edition of this poem, reach the high-water mark of lyrical composition. Few will deny that, taken together, the five melodies: 'As through the land,' 'Sweet and low,' 'The splendor falls on castle walls,' 'Home they brought her warrior dead,' and 'Ask me no more!'—that these constitute the finest group of songs produced in our century."

Should not Mr. Stedman have included "Tears, idle tears"?

133, 1015. **Phantom of the house.** The Banshee, a phantom that was supposed to shriek before a death in the family to which it was attached.

134, 1042–4. **So let me hence,** etc. Can you think of a deeper meaning that Tennyson may have had in these lines?

1047. **Fine.** What special significance here?

135, 1079–93. Why does Elaine refuse to believe the slander? Compare the Queen's jealous love.

138, 1160. **Diamonds.** What is the syntax?

1165–69. What do these lines show concerning the attitude of the court toward the Queen and Lancelot? Cf. l. 734.

139, 1178. **Tawnier than her cygnet's.** The cygnet or young swan has yellow or tan-colored down.

1183. **Rumors.** What rumors?

1197–1225. Does the Queen still acknowledge her love for Lancelot? Does she suffer more from wounded pride or from the thought of lost affection? How far has she thought out this interview beforehand? Why does the Queen say, "have your joys apart" (l. 1210)? What is the one thing she feels that she cannot do?

1201–4. Cf. 121 ff., also " Guinevere," 607–656.

140, 1206. **Your own.** Your own what?

1207–8. **The value of all gifts,** etc. Cf.

> To the noble mind
> Rich gifts wax poor when givers prove unkind.
> *Hamlet,* III, i, 100–1.

1209. **Fancy.** What peculiar force has this word here?

141, 1243–5. **The face that men shape,** etc. Read Hawthorne's " The Great Stone Face."

142, 1264–74. What dramatic purpose does Elaine's letter serve?

145, 1345–62. " It would seem as if the saddest thing in all Lancelot's life must have been his feeling toward Arthur. Had he (Lancelot) been wholly a traitor at heart, he would have despised him, or hated him, or both. But he still reveres him and still loves him."—TAINSH, *A Study of Tennyson's Works,* p. 218.

1354. **Homeless trouble.** Cf. 244–6. Arthur alone does not know the cause.

146, 1382–6. Does Lancelot feel that his sin is the cause of Elaine's death? Does he admit it to himself?

1386–90. Give the literal meaning. Does Lancelot really question the genuineness of the Queen's affection?

1389. Where have we seen " the crescent fear for name and fame " ?

147, 1405–7. Look for a parallel in " Guinevere."

1409–16. Compare the irresolution of Godfrey Cass in *Silas Marner.*

1412–16. Why is not this a proper prayer? Wherein does Lancelot fall short of true repentance? Cf. " Guinevere," 371–5, also *Hamlet,* III, iii, 36–72. Is Lancelot's remorse a permanent state of mind? Does it make for righteousness? What do you see in the last hundred lines that is worthy of comment? Write a paragraph giving from your own observation an illustration of the idea in ll. 1406–7.

THE HOLY GRAIL

For comments on "The Holy Grail" read Introduction, page 9, also *Tennyson, His Art and Relation to Modern Life,* by Stopford A. Brooke, page 319 ff., also page 300 ff.

149, 15. **Puffed . . . smoke.** The wind scattering the pollen of the yew-tree. Cf. *In Memoriam,* XXXIX.

150, 39. **Without.** What part of speech?

40. One of your own knights. Cf. lines 697–704.

48. Aromat. A poetic name for Arimathea, suggestive of the abundance of spices from that region.

49. Day of darkness. Cf. *Matthew*, XXVII, 52.

51. Arimathean Joseph. Cf. *Matthew*, XXVII, 57; also "Balin and Balan," 99, 100.

52. Winter thorn. "There is a variety of hawthorne which puts forth leaves and flowers about the time of Christmas. It is said to have originated at Glastonbury Abbey, and the original thorn was believed to have been the staff with which Joseph of Arimathea aided his steps on his wanderings from the Holy Land to Glastonbury, where he is said to have founded the celebrated Abbey."—W. J. ROLFE.

151, 80. Cf. "Guinevere," 484–490, also 75–82.

152, 93. **It.** What is the antecedent?

155, 178. **If I lose myself,** etc. Cf. *John*, XII, 25.

195. I sware a vow, etc. Cf. Lowell's "The Vision of Sir Launfal."

156, 209. **Crying on help.** Crying for help.

159, 286–327. In the vow to seek the Holy Grail and in the "strength and will to right the wronged" are typified the contrasting ideals of cloistered spiritual perfection and of social service. With which does Tennyson show the greater sympathy? Which is more prominent in the religious thought of to-day? Give examples of each type of present-day activity.

287. What go ye into the wilderness to see? Cf. *Matthew*, XI, 7.

298. The leader's bell. Follow like a flock of sheep.

160, 311. **Twelve great battles.** Cf. "Lancelot and Elaine," 285 ff.

333–337. Cf. Tennyson's poem, "Sir Galahad."

161, 358. **Gate.** Cf. "Gareth and Lynette," 209–226.

162, 377. **Thirsty.** Cf. *Matthew*, V, 6.

379–439. In this passage Tennyson portrays with marvelous poetic power some of the various interests of life. Percivale is thirsting for a spiritual perfection which is removed from contact with humanity. He finds,—

> All these things at once,
> Fell into dust, and I was left alone,
> And thirsting in a land of sand and thorns.

What interest is represented by each of the following passages: 379–390; 391–400; 401–420; 421–439? Do you agree with his ideal? What does Tennyson mean by the recurring passage, "fell into dust"?

380–383. Find other examples of Tennyson's descriptive power.

165, 456. What does this line mean?

461. What is the allegorical significance of this line?

463. **Holy elements.** Explain.

476–481. How has Galahad's attainment of the vision affected his service in the world?

166, 489–560. "This great and lofty vision of the glory of the pure spiritual life, refined and thrilled by heavenly holiness into full union with the world beyond the sense, and needing no death to enter into the perfect life, is done as no one has done this kind of work since Dante. It is made all the more vivid, and its unfitness for the common toil of goodness on this earth is shown, by the contrast which Tennyson immediately makes to it in the daily life of the poor monk Ambrosius, who knows naught of marvels, but is the providence of the little village near which he lives."—STOPFORD A. BROOKE.

167, 509. **Shoutings of all the sons of God.** Cf. *Job*, XXXVIII, 7.

168, 540–560. Cf. Lowell's poem, "The Search."

170, 612–630. Does the old monk approve of Percivale's adherence to his vow? Do you?

171, 638. **Mad.** Cf. "Lancelot and Elaine," 250–252.

172, 661. **Paynim amid their circles,** etc. Pagans living among their Druidical circles of huge stones surrounding an altar where victims were sacrificed.

667–669. Cf. Vivien's magnificent song of fire-worship in "Balin and Balan," 434–453.

173, 681. **The seven clear stars.** Ursa major or "the big dipper."

175, 735. **The quiet life.** Cf. 4.

738–747. What are vows to a Gawain? Why did he make the vow at first?

759. **Like him of Cana,** etc. Cf. *John*, II, 10.

176, 769–780. Compare the speech of the King in *Hamlet*, III, iii, 37–72, particularly the line,

> May one be pardon'd and retain the offence?

783. Cf. "Lancelot and Elaine," 1401–1415, and also note on 1412–1416. Stopford A. Brooke says: "Lancelot, who has made the vow to seek the vision of pure holiness and love, while his heart loves his sin, sees the Grail covered, but sees it as holy wrath and fire, as swift and stern condemnation . . . from which he swoons, blasted, and burnt, and blinded. . . . But where then, Tennyson asks, is spirituality to be found, where

pure holiness, and love which beholds the invisible kingdom. It is to be found where Arthur found it, in the midst of human life, in honest love of men, in doing our duty where God has placed us."

GUINEVERE

182. The Year-Cycle of the Idylls. " ' The Coming of Arthur ' is on the night of the new year; when he is wedded ' the world is white with May; ' on a summer night the vision of the Holy Grail appears; and the Last Tournament is in the ' yellowing autumn-tide.' Guinevere flees through the mists of autumn, and Arthur's death takes place at midnight in midwinter."— Tennyson's note in the *Memoir*, II, 133. Of course the time of the story covers many years.

2. **Almesbury.** Amesbury, near Salisbury. An abbey church still stands on the supposed site of an ancient British monastery.

183, 14. **With silent smiles,** etc. Cf. Pope's lines on Addison.

15. **Lord of the White Horse.** See note on L. E., 297.

16. **Hengist.** One of the Saxon chieftains who invaded Britain.

22. **Plumes that mocked the May.** White like hawthorn blossoms.

24. **All ear and eye.** Cf. L. E., 936.

184, 56. **I shudder,** etc. An old superstition. The Queen with a woman's intuition fears Modred.

62. **Modred's narrow foxy face.** Cf.

> Yond Cassius has a lean and hungry look;
> He thinks too much; such men are dangerous.
> *Julius Cæsar*, I, ii, 196.

64–91. **The Powers that tend the soul,** etc. Is Tennyson true to life in giving to the woman the firmer moral purpose? Has he heretofore shown Guinevere to be more troubled in conscience than Lancelot? Is her determination due to conscience or to fear?

74. **held.** What is the subject?

80. What is the significance of her shadow?

188, 166–77. See the parable of the ten virgins, *Matthew* XXV, 1–13.

190, 229–268. The child's talk is a recapitulation of the story of " The Coming of Arthur " as it may be supposed to have settled in the popular imagination.

" The solemn and fateful strain of the poems is for a moment relieved by a passage where with vigorous play of fancy and a just use of the preternatural, the merry life of the court and realm

of Arthur before guilt had come to taint it is described."—
W. E. GLADSTONE, *London Quarterly Review*, Oct., 1859.

191, 243–4. **Mermaiden, man-breasted things.** See Tennyson's poems, " The Merman," and " The Mermaid."

246–7. Cf. " The Bugle Song " in *The Princess*.

192, 289. **Bude and Bos.** Districts of Cornwall.

193, 294. **By miracle.** Arthur drew from a stone a sword that no other knight could move. *Morte D'Arthur*, I, 3.

300–305. Cf.

> I touch the chords of joy, but low
> And mournful answer notes of woe.
> > SCOTT, *The Lady of the Lake*, II, 124–5.

194, 334–4. Cf.

> For who can always act? but he,
> To whom a thousand memories call,
> Not being less but more than all
> The gentleness he seemed to be.
>
> Best seem'd the thing he was, and join'd
> Each office of the social hour
> To noble manners, as the flower
> And native growth of noble mind.
> > *In Memoriam*, CXI.

340. Why does the Queen continue to talk with the novice?

196, 370–5. **Surely I repent**, etc. Why is Guinevere's spiritual condition here healthier than Lancelot's in L. E., 1409–16?

375. What is the meaning of the repetition of the words, " to see him more "?

197, 405. Is the Queen honestly repentant?

419–523. Is there any part of this passage that you would omit? Do the King's ideals center around the kingdom or the home?

419–656. In those two superb speeches to his sinful wife, and in the Queen's lament beginning, " Gone—my lord! " Tennyson has risen to more sublime heights of poetry than elsewhere in the Idylls. There are many other beautiful passages, unsurpassed descriptions, subtle delineations of character,—

> jewels five-words-long
> That on the stretch'd forefinger of all Time
> Sparkle forever,

but nowhere is there a passage so sustained in dramatic interest, so truly pathetic, nor so charged with the deepest human sym-

pathy as this. Its effect is like that of the sleep-walking scene
in *Macbeth* after which the Doctor exclaims, " God, God forgive us all! "

199, 483. Has the Queen been jealous of the King's devotion
to his work? Cf. L. E., 129 ff., also note on L. E., 157.

201, 536. **Is past.** What is the subject?

537. **Pang.** What is its predicate?

202, 574. **Event.** Give the Latin derivation. Lines 419–523
show the King; 529–577, the man. Which passage is more ef-
fective? Why?

204, 624. **That.** What?

608–56. What is the one thought to which the Queen clings
as her hope of regeneration?

Arthur places the whole blame for the wreck of his home upon
Guinevere and she accepts it all. Do you agree that he is blame-
less?

205, 631. Cf. 370–75.

" No one, we are persuaded, can read this poem without feeling when it ends, what may be termed the pangs of vacancy—
of that void in heart and mind for want of its continuance of
which we are conscious when some noble strain of music ceases,
when some great work of Raphael passes from the view, when we
lose sight of some spot connected with high associations, or when
some transcendent character upon the page of history disappears,
and the withdrawal of it is like the withdrawal of the vital air."—
W. E. Gladstone, *London Quarterly Review*, Oct., 1859.

THE PASSING OF ARTHUR

208, 9–28. Arthur is puzzled by a world-old problem. He has
honestly striven " to work His will," and now he sees his efforts
overwhelmed by evil,—-

> I waged his wars, and now I pass and die.

In the midst of his despair, however, he sees one hope,—

> Perchance, because we see not to the close.

Cf. *Psalms*, LXXIII, 12–13.

12. **Pass.** Pass away; sometimes used as an equivalent for
die, again in an indefinite sense, as in 28.

209, 26. **Reels . . . beast.** Cf. " The Coming of Arthur,"
10–12.

33. **Hollow, hollow all delight.** Why should Gawain be the
one to bring this message?

The vague suggestiveness of this Idyll is one of the masterly touches of the poet. The ghostly message of Gawain with its sepulchral, " Hollow, hollow all delight," the simile of the " wild birds that wail their way from cloud to cloud," and the " last, dim, weird battle in the death-white mist " are all pervaded with the atmosphere of the inevitable hour, and with uncertain visions of the world to come. For the cultivation of responsiveness to the real essence of poetry there is no better means than the memorizing of such passages.

210, 68. **Brake the petty kings,** etc. Arthur was the first to unite the petty kings under one rule, and to repudiate the payment of tribute to Rome. Cf. " The Coming of Arthur," 5–19, also 504–13.

69. **The Roman wall** was a line of fortifications extending from the Solway to the Tyne to repel the Picts and Scots.

90–91. See note on the Year-Cycle, " Guinevere," p. 240.

212, 117. **Voices of the dead.** Cf. l. 103.

213, 155. **Call not . . . of my house.** Call not this traitor a member of my family.

157. Cf. *Matthew* XII, 50.

214, 170. This line is the beginning of Tennyson's early poem, *Morte D'Arthur*, published in 1842. " Balin and Balan," the last of *The Idylls of the King*, was published in 1885.

215, 191–2. **Merlin sware,** etc. Cf. " The Coming of Arthur," 418–23.

195–203. See note on G. L., 66.

197–201. **An arm rose up,** etc. Cf. " The Coming of Arthur," 294–308.

216, 233. **Strode he back slow.** Why *slow?*

238–9. Could the participles *lapping* and *washing* be interchanged without loss?

217, 256–77. Is this argument true to human nature?

262. **Obedience.** Cf. L. E., 713.

218, 278. **Clouded,** etc. Bedivere's sense of duty becomes clouded by his own arguments.

219, 301. Why *quickly* and *ran?*

221, 354–60. Note the contrast between the harsh and broken music of 354–8, and the liquid alliteration of 359–60.

222, 403. **Image of the mighty world.** " Also Merlin made the Round Table in tokening of the roundness of the world, for by the Round Table is the world signified by right."—Malory, *Morte D'Arthur*, Bk. XVI, ch. 2.

223, 427. **Avilion.** See note on G. L., 492.

428–31. Cf. *Isaiah*, XXXV, 9–10; also *Revelations*, XXI, 4.

469. **The new year.** See note on the Year-Cycle, " Guinevere," p. 240.

GLOSSARY

affiance . . .	L. E.	1346	trust
agaric . . .	G. L.	729	fungus. *See* foul fleshed
allow . . .	L. E.	201	pardon
allowed of .	L. E.	110	approved by
an			if (used often with this meaning)
anon . . .	G. L.	193	soon
Arthur's Harp	G. L.	1281	a constellation, probably the Great Bear
Avanturine .	G. L.	908	(a-van′tū rin) a variety of feldspar spangled with mica
avoid . . .	G. L.	733	go away
bar	G. L.	152	the buttery bar, across which food was handed from the kitchen
belike . . .	G. L.	697	likely
black-stoled .	P. A.	365	black robed
blazoned . .	G. L.	398	given in heraldic colors
boon . . .	G. L.	327	favor, privilege
braided . .	L. E.	8	embroidered
brake . . .	C. A.	39	broke, obsolete or poetic form
brand . . .	C. A.	119	sword, called *brand* from its flashing
brewis . . .	G. L.	447	broth
broach . . .	G. L.	476	spit, a small bar on which meats were roasted before an open fire
brook . . .	G. L.	287	endure
burns . . .	G. L.	90	streams
burthen . .	L. E.	898	the refrain of a song
but . . .	G. L.	104	only
casque . . .	G. L.	665	helmet
cate	G. L.	827	dainty viand
catiff . . .	G. L.	779	base, cowardly
charlock . .	G. L.	380	(char′lŏk) wild mustard
charm . . .	G. L.	84	allure
churl . . .	G. L.	419	low-born fellow
clomb . . .	G. L.	56	climbed, obsolete or poetic form

colewort	G.	32	cabbage
comb	G. L.	1163	a bowl-shaped hollow or valley enclosed on all sides but one by steep cliffs. *Cent. Dict.*
cuirass	L. E.	293	breastplate
cuisses	P. A.	383	armor for the thighs
divisings	G. L.	1314	skill, tactics
devoir	L. E.	118	duty, respectful notice
did their days in stone	G. L.	298	carved records of their deeds in stone
dole	G.	677	alms
dole	L. E.	1129	grief
donn'd	G. L.	675	put on
downs	L. E.	162	rolling land not covered by forests
dragon boughts	G. L.	229	coils of the dragons' tails
drave	G. L.	201	archaic past of *drive*
enow	C. A.	252	enough
evensong	G. L.	773	the time of evening service
fain	L. E.	767	glad
favor	L. E.	356	a gift from a maiden to her knight, worn by him in battle to show that he was fighting for her
for	C. A.	41	because
foul fleshed agaric	G. L.	729	ill smelling fungus
frontless	G. L.	839	shameless
gave upon	G. L.	651	opened upon
ghostly	L. E.	1092	spiritual
glamor	G. L.	202	enchantment
good lack	G. L.	105	a mild oath
grace	G. L.	951	favor
greaves	P. A.	383	armor for the lower part of the legs
guerdon	G. L.	810	reward
gyve and gag	G. L.	362	gyve, fetter; gag, a mouth covering which prevents speech. This is an allusion to the ducking stool used as a punishment for scolding women.
had	G. L.	366	would have, as often in Tennyson
haler	G.	679	healthier
hern	G. L.	1155	heron
Hesperus	G. L.	1174	evening star

hest	. .	P. A.	211	command
hold	. .	G. L.	584	stronghold
holden	. .	C. A.	213	held
holp	. .	C. A.	141	help. Obsolete, cf. holpen
holt	. .	G. L.	729	woods
housel	. .	G.	147	sacrament
instant	. .	G. L.	1318	urgent
jousts	. .	G. L.	85	(jŭsts) tournaments or mock battles
knaves	. .	G. L.	151	the old meaning of boys or servants. Cf. *Julius Cæsar* IV, 3, 270
leash	. .	G. L.	51	three. Three hounds were usually held by a single thong or leash. Hence the word came to be used for *three.*
Lent-lily	. .	G. L.	889	daffodil
lets	. .	L. E.	94	hinders
lief	. .	P. A.	248	beloved
lightly	. .	G. L.	934	quickly, a frequent use
lissome	. .	G.	28	lithesome
loon	. .	G. L.	751	stupid fellow
mage	. .	C. A.	279	magician
mavis	. .	G. L.	1052	thrush
mere	. .	G. L.	778	(mēr) a small stagnant lake or pool
Meridies	. .	G. L.	1174	midday
merle	. .	G. L.	1052	blackbird
meseems	. .	G. L.	832	obsolete or poetic for *it seems to me*
mien	. .	G. L.	443	appearance
Mors	. .	G. L.	1175	death
narrow seas	.	L. E.	1312	the English Channel
Nox	. .	G. L.	1175	night
of a doubt	.	P. A.	268	doubtful. Cf. "Thieves of mercy," *Hamlet* IV, 6, 18
offices	. .	P. A.	293	duties
oriel	. .	L. E.	1170	a window projecting from the wall and supported by brackets
part	. .	C. A.	392	depart. Cf. *pass*, L. E. 1084
pass	. .	L. E.	1084	die. See note on P. A. 12
Phosphorus	.	G. L.	1174	morning star
pricked	. .	G. L.	1190	spurred
puissance	. .	C. A.	17	power, strength
purport	. .	G. L.	603	purpose

quest	G. L.	535	search
quit	L. E.	939	reward
ramp	G. L.	1273	rear on hind legs
rathe	L. E.	338	early
reave	G. L.	411	deprive
roundelay	G. L.	496	a song containing a recurring line
ruth	G. L.	873	pity
samite	L. E.	431	(sam'ite) heavy silk cloth
scaur	L. E.	53	(skär) a steep slope or cliff
seized of	G. L.	351	possesses
seneschal	G. L.	359	old or chief servant
shoulder slipt	G. L.	740	with shoulder put out of joint
shrift	G.	147	absolution after confession
shrive	L. E.	1093	make confession and receive absolution
simples	L. E.	857	medical plants
slipt her at	L. E.	653	sent her to pursue
sometime	L. E.	1265	formerly
sooth	G. L.	1146	truth
sorcery	G. L.	201	magic
spate	G. L.	3	a sudden flood or freshet
spit	G. L.	771	a small bar on which meats were roasted before an open fire, here of course for *lance*
standeth seized of	G. L.	351	holds possession of
still	G. L. 176, L. E. 933, etc.		Tennyson uses this word frequently in the Elizabethan sense of *always*.
stoat	G. L.	871	ermine
straitn'd	L. E.	870	restrained, bound
tale	L. E.	91	count, number. Cf. tally, teller
tarns	G. L.	489	mountain lakes
tarriance	L. E.	567	delay
thrall	G. L.	162	one who runs errands, hence a servant or slave
throughly	G. L.	1372	an Elizabethan word used interchangeably for *thoroughly*
tinct	L. E.	10	color
trefoil	G. L.	1130	three-leaved clover
trick out	G. L.	1355	adorn, dress up
troth and fealty	G.	439	loyalty and allegiance
unhappiness	G. L.	749,	ill luck, mischance
unsolders	P. A.	182	disunites

vert	. . .	C. A.	274	green
villain	. . .	G. L.	157	one of the lowest social rank. An extremely interesting word. *See Cent. Dict.*
wan-sallow	.	G. L.	444	colorless
ward	. . .	G. L.	1072	place of guard
ware	. . .	P. A.	363	aware
weald	. . .	G.	127	wild. Sometimes applied to a section in the S. E. of England
wit	. . . .	C. A.	279	wisdom. Cf. the verb as, e. g., in L. E. 766
worship	. .	L. E.	1316	honor
wot	. . .	G. L.	1299	knows
yield	. . .	G. L.	18	reward, as often in Shakespeare

QUESTIONS AND TOPICS FOR STUDY

The following questions cover the general intent, moral purpose, character study, and present-day application of the Idylls. Some of them cannot be answered without studying the entire cycle of poems, and it is hoped that the use of these questions may encourage pupils to read the Idylls as a whole.

1. What is meant by the theme of a poem?
2. What is the theme of *The Idylls of the King?* (See Introduction, p. 15.)
3. Without reproducing the story, show the relation of each of the Idylls studied to the theme.
4. In the complete cycle, how does Tennyson make the transition from "Gareth and Lynette" to "Lancelot and Elaine" less abrupt? (See pp. 96–97.) Have you read the intervening poems?
5. Contrast the effect of the sin in the court upon individuals as shown in "The Marriage of Geraint" and "Geraint and Enid" on the one hand, and "Balin and Balan" and "Lancelot and Elaine" on the other.
6. If you have read "The Holy Grail," "Pelleas and Ettare," and "The Last Tournament," show the similarity in character between Gareth and Pelleas, and the contrast between the conditions in the court at the time of their coming.
7. What was the fundamental cause of the change in the court?
8. What would be the probable effect of the moral environment of the court in each period upon a young man of high ideals?
9. Name any Gareths you know in modern public life who have kept the ideal to "live pure, speak true, right wrong," etc.

10. Contrast the social ideals shown in "Gareth and Lynette" with those of to-day.

11. By references to "The Holy Grail" and to the other Idylls, give arguments for or against the proposition that Lancelot was sincere in his efforts to find the Holy Grail and to purify his soul.

12. Was Tennyson in sympathy with a person who seeks self-perfection by withdrawing from the world? (Read the last 18 lines of "The Holy Grail.")

13. Was Lancelot honestly devoted to Arthur and his work, in the first two Idylls?

14. How does Lancelot feel about his false excuse for not accompanying the King to the Tournament in "Lancelot and Elaine"?

15. Who shows the firmer moral sense in "Lancelot and Elaine," Lancelot or Guinevere?

16. In "Lancelot and Elaine," does Lancelot feel that he is wrecking the great purpose of the King? Support your answers by reference to the poems.

17. Wherein does Lancelot's soliloquy in "Lancelot and Elaine," ll. 1382–1416, fall short of true repentence? Has any man a right to make such a prayer as that in ll. 1412–1416? Give reasons for your answer.

18. Why are we not shocked by the violation of conventionality in Elaine's declaration of her love for Lancelot? Compare Miranda in Shakespeare's *The Tempest*, III, i.

19. Compare the manners of Lancelot and of Gawain at Astolat.

20. What was Gawain's single object in life? Can you name any similar characters in fiction? Have you known any real people of similar natures? What were the feelings of their associates toward them?

21. What special significance is there in the word *wandering* (C. A., l. 32)?

22. What significance is there in Gawain's final verdict on life (P. A., ll. 33–40)? How would Lancelot's verdict differ?

23. By reference to "Lancelot and Elaine," show Guinevere's

attitude toward the King's great purpose. Has she any reason for feeling less interest in it than Lancelot feels?

24. Do you blame Arthur for his absorption in the work of perfecting the kingdom? Wherein did he fail in his duty to Guinevere? Was this failure excusable?

25. Would the glory of the kingdom have brought any credit to Guinevere?

26. Was Arthur devoted to his work for personal or for philanthropic reasons?

27. Is there any suggestion in the Idylls that Tennyson saw any failure on Arthur's part?

28. Do you sympathize more with Arthur or with Guinevere?

29. What was the attitude of the knights towards Arthur's effort to cleanse the realm, in "The Coming of Arthur" and "Gareth and Lynette"? What changes in their attitude do you see in "Lancelot and Elaine," "The Last Tournament," and "Guinevere"?

30. What passages in the Idylls suggest Tennyson's religious belief? What was his attitude toward death?

31. By references to the poems, justify the statement that Tennyson has used a sixth-century historical setting, a mediæval chivalry, and nineteenth-century social ideals.

32. Name some of the most dramatic scenes in the poems.

33. Give some of the best descriptions of people. Of nature.

34. Repeat your favorite short passage; your favorite sustained passage; the part of the allegory that appeals to you most strongly.

35. Whom do you consider the most human character in the Idylls? Give reasons for your answer.

36. Has your attitude toward poetry been changed by the study of the Idylls? If it has, what is the nature of the change?

37. Do you intend to read again the Idylls studied?

38. Have you read *Enoch Arden, The Lotus Eaters, The Princess*? Do you know also Tennyson's *The Lady of Shalott, Sir Galahad, Sir Lancelot and Queen Guinevere*, and *In the Children's Hospital*?